BETTER
GOLF

THE SYSTEMATIC WAY

BETTER GOLF

THE SYSTEMATIC WAY

MIKE PALMER

Sterling Publishing Co., Inc.
New York

Acknowledgements

Thanks to the East Sussex National Golf Club, Uckfield, Sussex for use of their excellent facilities, especially to Greg Dukart, Director of Golf.

The photographs on pages 20, 21, 22 and 23 were supplied courtesy of Titleist, those on pages 24 and 25 by Apollo. The photograph on pages 26 and 27 was supplied by Aldila. All the remaining photographs were taken by Keith Hailey at East Sussex National Golf Club near Uckfield.

Golf clubs by Sayers of Scotland.

Glove by Kasco.

Shoes by Cotswold Golf of Gloucester.

Clothing by Lyle and Scott, Hawick, Scotland.

1 3 5 7 9 10 8 6 4 2

Library of Congress Cataloging-In-Publication Data

Palmer, Mike.

Better Golf: the systematic way/Mike Palmer.

p.   cm.

First published in Great Britain by Hamlyn an imprint of Reed Consumer Books Limited under the title *Advanced Systematic Golf*

Includes index

ISBN 0-8069-0980-3

1. Golf. I. Title

GV965. P37   1995   94-25147

796.352—dc20   CIP

Published 1995 by Sterling Publishing Company, Inc.

387 Park Avenue South, New York, N.Y. 10016

©1995 by Reed International Books Limited

Distributed in Canada by Sterling Publishing

c/o Canadian Manda Group, One Atlantic Avenue, Suite 105

Toronto, Ontario, Canada M6K 3E7

Printed and bound in Hong Kong

ISBN 0-8069-0980-3

Contents

Foreword

Mike Palmer is the first to admit that golf is a difficult game to master, but he also believes that it isn't nearly as hard as it is sometimes made out to be.

Palmer is one of a new breed of PGA professionals who believe a structured approach is needed to learn the intricacies of golf. He provides this structure both in his earlier book, *Systematic Golf* (published in 1993), and in this book, which is designed as a refresher course for golfers who have mastered the basic skills, but still want to improve their game.

Within the pages of this ambitious new book, Palmer sets out to show us how to build on the basics to achieve better scores, and it is a measure of his success that he puts his message over without recourse to the unfathomable scientific jargon which less able teachers employ.

The author doesn't hide the difficulties of the game, but he still manages to explain things in a manner which reassures the reader and suggests he might have made a good academic had he not decided to devote his time and energy to the game he loves.

Palmer might not have the high profile of the more famous modern teaching gurus, but that should be attributed, not to his inadequacies as a teacher, but to his decision to devote his time to teaching true amateur golfers rather than top Tour stars.

Mike told me that at one stage of his career he gave lessons to more than 100 amateur golfers each week. This must have been tremendously hard work, and it was surely at this time that he gained the insight into the average golfer's problems which is so clear in this book.

Colin Callander
Editor *Golf Monthly*

Introduction

Golf is a very difficult game. It has many different facets to learn, practise and, hopefully, master. The full swing technique is just one aspect. You must then add to this: putting, chipping, pitching and bunker play. When these skills are learnt you then have to adapt them to suit different courses and weather conditions. You must select the right club for distance, assessing the effects of wind and ground conditions. You must plot your way around the course, avoiding losing balls, out of bounds and water hazards.

You will need knowledge of the basic rules, and a comprehensive understanding of golfing etiquette. You must maintain concentration for

1. A sound technique from the tee can mean the difference between powerful, accurate drives and embarassing lost balls.

eighteen holes, always sticking to a routine. You must be able to handle the bad shots and be capable of returning a good score even under the strains of competitive pressure.

Mastering the full swing is difficult enough. The ball is just 1.68 inches (43 mm) in diameter and the hitting face of your club has little room for error. The clubface must strike the back of the ball beneath its 'equator', but a touch too low will catch turf, slowing the clubhead speed and smothering the contact. Clearly, your swing must be precise.

Golf is unusual in that you strike a stationary ball. The vast majority of sports are moving ball sports. Golf is less dependent on good reflexes, more on good technique. In many sports, adherence to a 'text book' action is desirable – in golf, good technique is essential. Don't, however, be misled into believing the 'perfect' swing exists. Watching top professionals play, you will observe a whole variety of actions: quick, slow and rhythmical, long, short, flat, upright, hard hitting, orthodox and 'individual'. These differences bother many golfers, especially those who are analytical in their approach. However, amongst the varied swings seen, there are common features that should form the basis of learning for every golfer, whatever his or her standard. This forms what is described throughout this book as the 'model swing'. It is arrived at by breaking the swing action down into stationary positions which can be analyzed, checked and practised until familiar. All that remains is to assemble these swing positions, linking them together to create swing motion, resulting in clubhead speed at impact.

We all play golf for enjoyment. Even ambitious players striving for excellence can derive a great deal of fun from the challenge of the game. However, you must prepare to be humbled by the game at times: even the world's best occasionally play shots that are plain awful. We have all missed short putts and will again in the future, but you can take steps to hole the vast majority by adhering to a sound technique and practising it until grooved.

In your analysis and self-appraisal, be realistic about your approach to playing the game. The difficult nature of golf demands at least some practice in order to maintain a reasonable level of play, in which you

2. Bunker shots should be an important part of every golfer's practice sessions.

3. Experiment with a variety of shots to develop your range of shotmaking skills.

keep the swing movements repetitive and retain the necessary 'feel' for the shorter shots around and on the green.

When asked to advise golfers how to derive most fun from golf irrespective of their ability, I recommend the following:

i) Find a skilled instructor, identify a programme for swing technique and short game development and set realistic goals based on your enthusiasm, skill level and the amount of time you are able to devote to the game.

ii) Set aside time for constructive practice, working with positive ideas developed in conjunction with your instructor.

iii) Develop your overall knowledge of the game by reading magazines and books.

iv) Watch skilled golfers by attending tournaments. Copy their practice routines, focus on their swing repetition and how they manage their abilities out on the course.

v) Identify exactly why you play golf and organize accordingly. If you play purely for recreation, find others seeking the same and don't be forced into competitive events.

vi) Learn the basic rules of golf without having to refer to the rule book. For instance, know your options from a water hazard, the rule for playing a provisional ball should there be a possibility that your original ball is lost or out of bounds, and how to proceed if your ball is next to a staked tree.

vii) Know golf etiquette thoroughly.

Use good equipment, preferably from a reputable manufacturer, customized for your individual build or ability level. However, keep everything in perspective. A skilled player with a basic half set will always beat the player hoping to 'buy a better game'.

Accept that the game is somewhat elusive for everyone. Learning to handle bad shots is as important as enjoying and reflecting on your best. The perfect round of golf has never been played, and never will be. There is always scope for improvement.

Ultimately, the enjoyment you get out of the game of golf is dependent upon what you put into it. Learn, practise, play and have fun.

Mike Palmer

The Right Approach

HOW TO IMPROVE YOUR GOLF SCORES

The desire to achieve sustained improvement at golf is universal. A great score over 18 holes, one great hole or just a single well thought out, solid shot brings immense satisfaction. Golf is not the easiest game to master and, if you think you have achieved mastery, it is frequently short lived. It's not enough to practise and play often. Learning or improving at golf requires more than beating away practice balls. It has much more to do with creating a learning environment, a situation from which you can progress with a minimum of effort and maximum of results.

The mental side of the game is grossly underrated. Swing mechanics, minor tips and instruction are easier to take on board, but consider one point – you cannot set a swing in motion until the brain has programmed the body to perform in a particular way.

For example, when you learn to drive a car there seem so many considerations – gears, mirrors, speed limits, position in the road and so on. In time, intense concentration is no longer necessary as you have formed habits which are continuously monitored and instantaneously checked by the human brain. If you apply the same idea to golf, intense concentration is undesirable, awareness is important. Once learned, it is unnecessary to think hard about each and every swing. The habits are already formed.

1. Analyse your scores after each round, count your putts and focus upon areas that you can improve.

2. Warm your muscles properly before every round, or practice session, by swinging two clubs together.

3. Approach every shot from behind the ball-to-target line. Take time to picture the ideal flight for the ball.

3

mechanics of the various swings out on the course, but your overall impression is more important. If you had no knowledge of the golf swing, you would then copy what you had seen. If a teaching professional then briefly covered the basics of aim, grip, body alignment and posture, you would probably swing in a fairly orthodox manner. The strength is based on the picture you build up when watching the swings of professional players.

Why is this important? Simply because you cannot expect to achieve any constructive results without building on your observations and using your imagination. It's pointless finding the time to practise unless you do so in an effective manner. If you have no goals, no ideas and no objectives, the time will be at best wasted, even counter-productive.

CHECKPOINTS

● Practice for the sake of it will not necessarily produce results.
....
● You need a picture of what you are trying to achieve. Visualize the ball flight and sense the swing required.
....
● Build as many routines as possible into your golf game, particularly when assessing the shot and setting up to swing.
....
● The best, most efficient way to learn golf is to mimic good golfers.
....
● If you practise good basics, your game will progress steadily.

Strength of habit should be developed once your routine is correct. The greater the desire to play well, especially under competitive pressure, the more essential it is to have a programmed mind and body. Build as many routines as possible into both your practice sessions and your performances on the course. Repetition should be a key objective.

Human beings learn very efficiently by imitation. If you were to attend a tournament and watch good golfers, your brain would soak up the technique required and you would even sense how their swings feel. The swings look comfortable, rhythmic and seemingly lack physical effort; the ball flight is long and straight. You can't identify the

EFFECTIVE PRACTICE

Few golfers practise efficiently. Those who do use their time well, spread their practice to cover all aspects in an organized manner. They warm up beforehand, start with lofted irons and progress to the driver. Most of these players have a skilled professional whom they periodically consult to appraise and advise on all aspects of their game. These golfers are well known at every club as they invariably have low handicaps, play off scratch or are professionals.

The golf swing requires repetition of a fairly complex series of positions and motions. Practice is split into three main sections:

i) Learning practice. Developing an idea, swing concept or technique will require practice to identify how it will look and feel to you. This is most important when comparing it to a swing habit that you are trying to eliminate.

ii) Maintenance practice. Assuming your swing technique is sound, you will need to recognize movements which, while not requiring major adjustment, will need occasional fine tuning.

iii) Repetition practice. A golf swing that is to work under tournament pressure, especially at the highest levels, must be repetitive as well as technically sound. This demands a high volume of golf shots hit on the practice ground to build the swing to peak performance, rather as a racing car engine being tinkered with to provide that extra boost.

There are several key pointers to effective practice. If you are serious about your golf and seek a gradual and sustained improvement, you should adhere to each of these:

i) Find a level area from which to hit balls. The ground should be firm, the grass short and every ball played from a clean lie. Try to practise in milder weather rather than in the uncomfortable extremes of heat or cold. Use good quality practice balls that closely match or are identical to those you play with on the course. Keep them clean and reject those which are badly scuffed or damaged. Visit golf ranges which stock quality balls and have mats that best mimic the texture of fine grass.

ii) Make sure you always warm up properly before hitting any full practice shots. Either place a club behind your shoulders, turning back

1. Constant revision of the basics is the key to consistent improvement. Check the golf ball position – ideally it should be one clubhead's width inside the left heel.

and through in a similar manner to the swing pivot to free the major golfing muscles, or, alternatively, build up gradually from short swings with a lofted club.

iii) Isolate your objectives and key thoughts. Fresh, constructive ideas usually originate from golf instruction, especially if combined with viewing your swing action on video.

iv) Allocate your time according to the demands of all sections of the game. For most skilled golfers, some 60% of all shots will be from less than 100 yards (90m). Only 40% will require a full swing. Between 40 and 43% of strokes will be putts. You will only use your driver perhaps 13 or 14 times per round.

v) Take time to think through each shot. Pick a target to aim at, and visualize the ball flight and the swing technique required to reach it.

2

Take practice swings to familiarize yourself with the shot ahead. Position your other practice balls well away from the ball to be played; by doing this you will avoid any rapid-fire tendency. Assess the results and adjust accordingly. In short, practise as you would play out on the course, as this is by far the most useful and constructive approach to practice.

2. Develop your 'touch and feel' shots by practising a variety of lofted shots onto the practice green. Skilled golfers should vary club selection and experiment with different amounts of loft and roll on the ball. Monitor your results carefully and adjust your shots accordingly.

POSITIVE SWING CONCEPTS

When reviewing your swing, it is essential you have a clear picture of how it works. The following four-point swing revision identifies the movements which collectively form the completed swing action.

1. START WITH POSTURE AND ALIGNMENT Leave the club on the ground, open your feet out at shoulders' width and align your body parallel to the target line. Tilt your upper body forwards, pushing your bottom out and flexing your knees a touch to assist

swing stability. Let your arms hang down from your shoulders, without any tension, keeping both palms facing towards one another. Now set your body turn in motion by swinging back and through, your extending left arm going back whilst your right folds away, mostly downwards but also towards your side. Fold your right wrist back on itself as the arms reach hip height. Now reverse this and mirror it on the other side, most importantly permitting your left arm to fold towards your body. Encourage weight shift to the target side by raising your right heel as you pass the impact position. Note the mirror imaging in the swing, extending left arm going back, crossing over to right arm extension in the forward movement.

2. ADD THE GRIP AND CLUBFACE CONTROL Return to your address position alignment and posture, now adding the club. Your hands must be placed in a 'neutral' position on the club, left hand revealing two and a half knuckles, palm of your right hand facing the target. Whether you overlap, interlock or place all fingers on the club is not important, but maintain a light grip pressure to keep the muscles free enough to swing with rhythm.

Swing back and through as before, but focus on the clubface position at halfway back. The leading edge will be directed at 11.30 on an imaginary clock face. Mirror image this on the other side, feeling your arms rotate over to direct the toe end skywards.

As the swing moves back and through, introduce a positive weight transference. The weight shifts in the direction you are swinging the club, but keep your left heel down going back, whilst encouraging your right to lift past the impact position.

3. ADD SWING LENGTH AND WRIST ANGLES The basics are in place, so simply extend the swing either side, left arm swinging the club up as the backswing progresses. The shaft will find a position over the joint of your right shoulder, preserving a straightish line across the back of your left hand running into your forearm. This keeps the clubface square. The back of your right hand will form a concave shape, folding back on itself and locating under the shaft at the top of the backswing. Swing down and mirror image this on the other side.

4. PIVOT TO ADD POWER The pivot describes the upper body turn and lower body resistance which occurs in every good swing action. Turn your right side out of the way going back, whilst angling your left shoulder towards the ball so your spine angle remains constant. Really stretch the muscles across your back as the backswing nears completion, triggering a reversal of the swing in sequence. In the follow-through, turn your left side fully until the left leg straightens, but again keep your right shoulder low. The pivot shapes the golf swing, it ensures that the arms and club move gradually to the inside path going back, resulting in the club shaft being positioned over the joint of the right shoulder at the top. Try to feel comfortable, in control and balanced.

MYTHS AND MISCONCEPTIONS

To sustain improvement, you must have an understanding of the fundamentals, and practise them until they are grooved into place. Many golfers fall at the first hurdle by adhering to less important, even incorrect swing concepts. Here are some of those golfing myths:

keep their left arm straight, do so to extremes, locking it rigidly at the set-up and creating unwanted tension. As the club approaches impact, the left arm dominates, preventing the right hand and lower arm releasing. The clubface arrives open at the ball causing a slice.

KEEP YOUR LEFT ARM STRAIGHT No! The terminology is misleading. The left arm should be comfortably extended at the address position. Throughout the backswing and downswing, it maintains swing radius by remaining extended. Past impact, the right arm takes over, permitting the left to gradually fold away. Most golfers, when told to

KEEP YOUR HEAD DOWN All ball sports require the eyes to focus on the object to be hit. Quite naturally, your head will stay down long enough, assuming the swing is fundamentally sound. Topping occurs when the upper body lifts out of posture, forcing the head upwards. This is not head up; this is failure to maintain the spine angle. The head is forced upwards, and no amount of trying to 'keep your head down' will solve this. The opposite is usually more applicable. Try to keep your head up, sitting high on your shoulders, not buried into your chest, to permit freedom to pivot fully both back and through.

KEEP YOUR HEAD STILL Your lower spine is, in fact, the swing centre and it is this area that should remain stationary throughout. Your head is not, as many people think, your swing centre. It need not remain still as you swing but should instead follow the turning action of the upper body which involves a weight shift. As you swing back, the head will certainly rotate in response to the turning of the shoulders. Far more likely, it will actually move to your right side as the weight transference and shoulder turn combine in the backswing. Keeping your head still can lead to a reverse pivot, whereby your weight shifts to your left side going back before moving to the right early in the downswing. The results of this can be disastrous.

SWING STRAIGHT BACK The path along which the clubhead travels is elliptical, both in the early part of the backswing and through the hitting area. As the swing moves on its most natural shape, dictated by the pivoting of the shoulders, the clubhead conforms to this 'inside path'. If you attempt to fight this most natural of swing shapes by forcing the clubhead straight back early in the backswing, it won't necessarily improve the path of the clubhead through impact. Instead you are likely to cause problems by allowing the arms to follow an artificially straight path back whilst the shoulders are trying to turn.

CHECKPOINTS

● Keeping your left arm straight introduces excessive tension, resulting in the clubface staying open at impact.

● It is unnecessary to keep your head down. Your eyes should instead focus on the ball, with your chin kept away from your chest.

● Your head must be permitted to rotate and even move laterally. Keeping your head still is too restrictive.

● Allow the clubhead to move around your right side going back – your upper body turn dictates that it should not go straight back.

1. Your left arm does not need to be rigid. Throughout the backswing it should remain extended, but past impact the right arm becomes dominant enabling the left arm to fold away.

2. Keep your head up and away from your chest at the address position and throughout the swing. This position permits a free turn of the shoulders towards the right side going back, and also encourages the arms to swing upwards in the second half of the backswing. Keeping your head down, as is so often advised, can restrict the turn of the shoulders.

3. The turn of the right shoulder to the right side early into the backswing dictates the round shape of the swing. The golf shaft should appear behind the player's right shoulder at this position. In this example the club has been forced straight back from the ball with relatively little turn of the shoulders.

MYTHS AND MISCONCEPTIONS (CONTINUED)

DEVELOP A 'LATE HIT' Action photography of tournament professionals can be misleading with regard to the golf swing and its source of power. Many golfers believe that the release or uncocking of the wrists must be delayed as long as possible in order to preserve power until the last moment. This is immediately followed, presumably, by an unleashing of this potential energy with the wrists and hands to square the clubface up for impact. A 'late hit' promotes an open clubface at impact and often encourages a slice.

SWING SLOWLY 'Swing slowly' is a popular, and in certain cases perfectly valid, piece of golfing advice. Many players rush when under competitive pressure and would do well to slow down. However, swing speed (tempo) is individual. A brisk, business-like swing may be ideal for one player whilst a very slow, lazy looking swing suits another. The overall pace of the swing is principally dictated by the time it takes to turn the shoulders 90 degrees in the backswing, reverse this and turn

120 degrees in the follow-through. The time it takes to complete this process varies from player to player. If you limit clubhead speed by constantly telling yourself to 'slow down', you will hit the ball shorter than your potential.

LEGS CREATE POWER Power in the golf swing principally comes from combining a good upper body turn with a free swinging action of the arms and club. Good weight distribution throughout is also required to assist with balance, but the legs contribute relatively little to the distance the ball travels. Their role is more related to supporting the pivoting of the upper body rather than creating power themselves.

PUTTING IS HALF THE GAME You would have to excel at your long game and have serious putting problems if this were true. Putting is 42–43% of the game at most ability levels – a useful statistic to note when analyzing your overall game to set goals for future practice.

1

2

3

OUTSIDE-TO-INSIDE SWING CAUSES A SLICE A sliced shot curves away to the right once its velocity has eased. The ball picks up sidespin due to an open clubface at impact. Once the golfer anticipates the slice, he finds that a swing which moves left through impact reduces the error. Now the ball takes off left or straight, but the slice stays on the fairway or finds less trouble. The swing moves across the line, from outside-to-inside, to compensate for the open clubface that causes the slice.

TOE END UP AT HALFWAY BACK This indicates a first part to the backswing with excessive rolling of the wrists. A neutral or square clubface at halfway back, shaft horizontal, would point the leading edge at between 11.00 and 11.30 on an imaginary clock face.

CHECKPOINTS

● The 'late hit' won't necessarily add to clubhead speed and will probably produce a slice.

● Find a swing speed to suit you, one which maximizes clubhead speed at impact, but don't stick rigidly to 'swinging slowly'.

● Your legs must support your upper body pivot. They don't in themselves influence clubhead speed.

● 'Toe end up' is incorrect. It encourages too much wrist rotation early in the backswing.

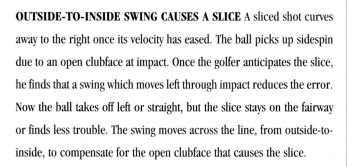

1. The club lags into the hitting area, and at hip height the wrists begin to release, producing an earlier hit than most golfers anticipate.

2 & 3. Legs don't create power, they merely support the upper body turn.

Equipment

THE GOLF BALL

Whether you are a fiercely competitive golfer, or just play for fun and exercise, you should carefully consider the type of golf ball you use. Golf balls are definitely not all the same, and every golfer should understand the differences. Once you have established which you prefer, stick to that one brand or something similar.

The ball which spins little for tee shots but maximizes spin for shots to the green, which limits side spin to minimize the extent of hooks and slices, which is soft and controllable for shots around the greens while offering durability when topped, is simply not available. Manufacturers meet the demands of golfers at all ability levels, but you have to identify the features you require.

Many golfers are totally unaware that the Rules of Golf place limitations on the size, weight and performance of golf balls. The key rules relate to initial velocity and overall distance. Under controlled conditions, all golf balls must not exceed a specified distance when driven so that they conform to a standard and can be used in competition.

COMPRESSION The golf ball's resistance to deformation is known as its compression. Usually marked on the box and the ball itself, compression is normally rated 80, 90 or 100, the latter being the hardest. Manufacturers regulate the compression by altering the core material formulation in a two-piece ball, or by adjusting the tension of the elastic winding in the wound ball. Since 'feel' and compression go together, you should change the

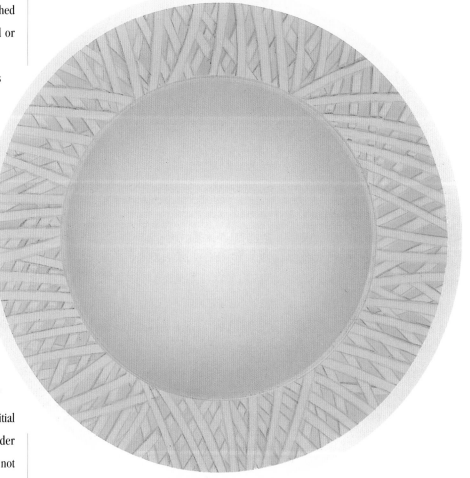

1. Wound Surlyn balls have a solid rubber centre, made from rubber windings encased in Surlyn.

2. The primary and secondary components of a balata covered ball.

compression according to the conditions. On colder days, try a lower rating; on very warm days, consider one that is higher.

TWO-PIECE OR WOUND There are three categories of construction: one-piece, two-piece and wound. One-piece balls are an insignificant sector of the market, used where low cost is more important than performance. Two-piece rightly represent the highest percentage of the market, with retail prices which make them affordable to most, whereas the wound ball is more expensive due to increased manufacturing costs. The two-piece

ball is manufactured from a moulded rubber core with various additives to control the final weight and compression. The cover material is injected around or compression moulded onto the core. Two-piece balls feel harder than wound, and generally fly lower. They also tend to bounce and run furthest, giving your shots greater distance.

Wound balls start with either a solid core or a rubber sac filled with a liquid or paste. The latter must be frozen in liquid nitrogen before its winding of elastic is added. The ball is encased by compression moulding two halves of the cover, printing and spray

lacquering. This ball is the obvious choice of the better golfer. The spin rate is greater than with the equivalent two-piece ball, but more significantly, the ball tends to leave the clubface on a lower trajectory and to peak later. Off the tee, its carry distance to the first bounce is similar to a two-piece. With irons, there will be a shorter carry and less bounce and roll, but greater control. The iron shots peak later and therefore land more softly from a steeper trajectory. If you want control more than distance and a soft landing which maximizes backspin, the wound ball should be your choice.

THE GOLF BALL (CONTINUED)

1. The different elements of a two-piece golf ball including raw Surlyn pellets.

COVER MATERIAL All two-piece and most wound golf balls are covered with a thin outer surface of thermoplastic resin called an ionomer. The most commonly used is Surlyn. This is available in many grades but most manufacturers, for top-grade balls, select Lithium Surlyn, its very tight molecular structure permitting a thinner cover whilst still being cut-proof.

Surlyn is a hard material, offering relatively little 'feel' off the clubface, though if combined with a softer core or wound centre, the combination can be perfectly suitable for better golfers. It has limited flexibility at impact, flattening relatively little and picking up backspin, though not as much as balata-covered balls. If you are inaccurate, this is the cover material that you should opt for. If the ball accepts a limited backspin rate, it will also limit sidespin, thereby restricting the amount it will hook and slice. Combined with a solid core, this is the ball for maximum distance. In general, the lower backspin rate and high compression combines to give a more parabolic flight (initially higher, descending flatter), maximizing the ball's bounce and roll, and hence its distance.

Wound balls are manufactured with either a Surlyn or balata cover. Originally a natural rubber but now synthetic, balata is softer, less durable and more susceptible to abrasion. A topped iron shot will cut or ripple this cover.

2. Titleist's cuboctahedron design has 440 dimples in eleven different sizes.

CHECKPOINTS

● Having chosen the brand of ball which most closely matches your requirements, stick to it.

● Always buy new golf balls, not production-line rejects or balls recovered from water hazards and resold.

● Experiment. Balancing the pros and cons of spin rate, 'feel' and distance can only be done by testing out a variety of balls.

● Golf balls can lose their shape. Change your golf ball at least as often as each 18 holes of competitive play.

This ball should be the choice of the low-handicap player who appreciates the enhanced feel and control. The softer balata cover responds more at impact, flattening against the face and imparting more backspin. It's simple enough: balata equals more spin, but don't think this always advantageous. If a balata-covered ball picks up more backspin, it will additionally pick up increased sidespin due to an open or closed clubface. If you already slice or hook, this is definitely not the ball for you, but if you are skilled enough it will enhance your shotmaking skills.

Putting, chipping and pitching are easier with a balata-covered ball. It permits a positive strike, really accelerating through the hitting area as the impact is relatively soft. Advantageous on fast hard greens.

For longer shots hit into greens, there is always a desire to have a high-spinning ball which will stop more quickly, especially when the landing area is hard during summer months. Since greater spin, control and 'feel' are, in the main, desirable to experienced players who already have distance in their shots, this cover material has a limited, though important, market.

Recent advances in cover material and dimple patterns are closing the gap between the spin rates of Surlyn and balata. In addition, the slightly higher manufacturing costs of the balata-covered ball mean the retail price difference is difficult for some golfers to justify, particularly when the limited life of a balata-covered ball, due to surface abrasion, is considered.

THE GOLF SHAFT

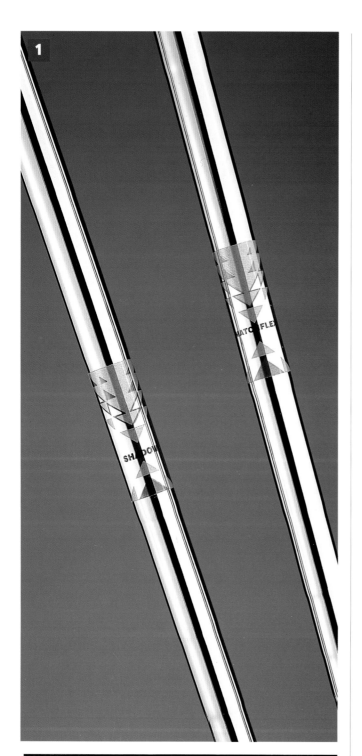

1. Steel shafts remain popular with many players, the examples here are by Apollo.

Choosing the correct shaft for your game is unquestionably one of the most important club decisions to be made. Consider the precise role of the shaft. It produces no power itself, but transmits it to the clubhead. As you swing, it flexes. In the perfectly timed shot, the clubhead will lag in the downswing but the clubhead mass catches up to overtake fractionally the centre line of the shaft on impact. The stored-up energy is delivered at this precise moment of impact. The shaft, therefore, depends on your timing to produce perfectly straight shots launched at the optimum trajectory.

There are many materials suitable for shafts, but two dominate: steel and graphite. Weight should be a major consideration. Steel shafts are available in conventional and light weight. If the shaft is lighter, the manufacturer can select fractionally heavier clubheads which will position greater mass behind the ball at impact.

For the average golfer, this translates into more distance because the lighter club is faster to swing. Though distance gains are limited, performance gains from lightweight steel are significant, though ultimately the material has limitations.

Not so with graphite. This has resulted in a rapid move forward in golf club technology. However, the complexities of correct selection of graphite shafts pose the greatest problem, as the playing characteristics can be altered so significantly. This is the principal difference between steel and graphite. Golfers who have tried graphite and preferred steel shafts have almost invariably tried the wrong graphite shaft. Steel shaft designs are limited by the fact that steel has multi-directional strength. The wall thickness and diameter of the shaft dictates the flexibility. Graphite, in contrast, is a very fine fibre, and can be arranged in the shaft construction to alter the characteristics of the flex and torque.

Key factors when looking for the best shafts for your game are:

MATERIAL Most shafts are steel and graphite, but some manufacturers use titanium. The shaft material must be your first consideration, as quality graphite is more expensive. Graphite is generally lighter than steel, permitting more mass in the clubhead, whilst making the overall weight of the club lighter, permitting it to be swung faster.

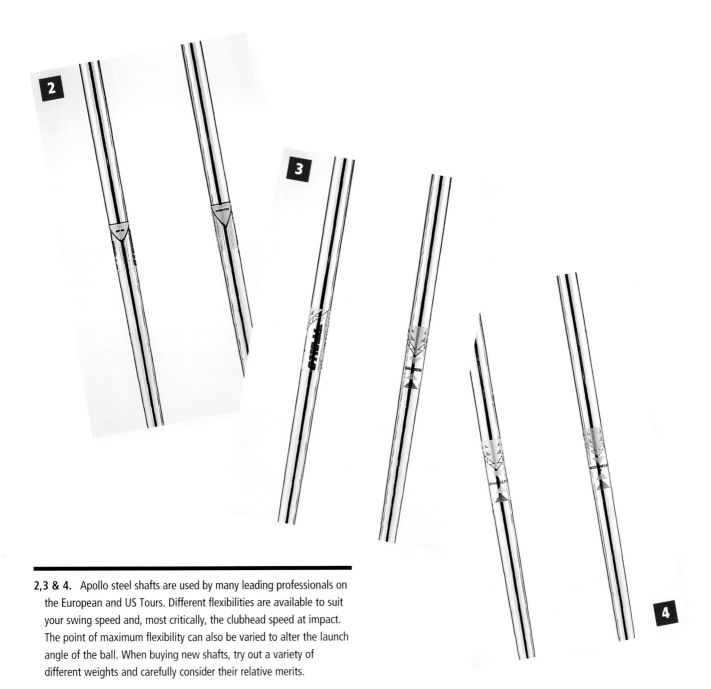

2,3 & 4. Apollo steel shafts are used by many leading professionals on the European and US Tours. Different flexibilities are available to suit your swing speed and, most critically, the clubhead speed at impact. The point of maximum flexibility can also be varied to alter the launch angle of the ball. When buying new shafts, try out a variety of different weights and carefully consider their relative merits.

If you are a decent player and you take your game seriously, don't bother trying low-priced graphite, but instead look at lightweight steel shafts. Early graphite shafts from the mid-1970s required a slower swing to time the unloading of the flex correctly. In contrast, a modern graphite club should be swung at your regular speed. If the club dictates a swing adjustment, you have the wrong shafts fitted. Remember, too, that you cannot simply switch shafts without it affecting other specifications. Changing your existing clubs from steel to graphite requires additional weight to be added to the clubheads.

The most common reason for golfers choosing graphite is to give their shots more distance. Whilst it is true that many golfers drive the ball further when using graphite shafts, there are other reasons why this material has become so popular.

Don't assume that graphite shafts are only for better golfers, or those who can justify the additional cost. Every golfer should be looking at this shaft material for a combination of reasons – it can offer greater distance and better 'feel' to your shots, greatly improved vibration absorption and ease of swing.

THE GOLF SHAFT (CONTINUED)

FLEX With steel, the thickness of the shaft dictates its stiffness. You simply match the flexibility to the clubhead speed you are generating. The correct flex will hit straight shots on the optimum trajectory. Too flexible a shaft will create inconsistency at impact, generally adding height to the shot and tending to draw it left of target. Too stiff a shaft leaves the ball out right and loses distance. Most male golfers should select regular flex shafts, with stiffer flexes more suitable for stronger and low-handicap players.

With graphite, the choice is far more complex, and confusing. There are numerous computations of flexibility and torque, and there is no industry standard to offer guidance.

TORQUE Torque is the measure of shaft twist. The torque rating is primarily reserved for graphite shafts and, used in conjunction with the flexibility, it helps identify the best shaft for you. Put simply, the more flexible the shaft, the more torque it will have. Stronger players generating plenty of clubhead speed require a stiffer flex shaft which consequently will have a lower torque rating.

KICK POINT The shaft has a kick point, at which the maximum deviation from straight is located between clubhead and grip. The limitations of steel as a material permit only mild variations in the kick point. The weaker golfer is assisted by the reduction of the wall thickness in the lower section of the shaft to give more tip flexibility. The lower kick point gives more height to the shot. Generally, stronger golfers need shafts with a higher kick point, reducing the action of the clubhead to give more control.

With graphite, design limitations are less constrained because the graphite fibres can be arranged in a multitude of ways to produce a wide range of specifications in the finished shaft. With the correct shaft fitted, lady golfers generating relatively slow clubhead speeds can gain height and distance. There is additionally improved 'feel' from the strike. Lower handicappers should also be able to produce better launch angles for the ball, controlling the flight.

SELECTION AND CARE OF GRAPHITE SHAFTS Most golfers starting out with a graphite-shafted driver have visions of more distance from the

tee. Some players instantly realise the advantages of graphite, which isn't necessarily longer drives. Make the most of facilities that have trial clubs, where you can experiment with both irons and woods. Don't assume all graphite is the same and narrow your options to one brand, but instead try out three or four different specifications.

Graphite shafts represent one of the most important advances in golf equipment. Early carbon fibre versions, first seen in the mid-1970s were widely tried and tested by a combination of club golfers and tournament professionals alike, but relatively few players were able to control the increased flex and and torque of the new shafts.

More recent design and production techniques have made graphite shafts a great deal easier to use. The result of these new improved graphite shafts is better performances – usually more distance. The proof of the performance of graphite is reflected in the growing number of tournament players worldwide who have moved away from steel shafts. The shift towards graphite shafts is most marked with regard to the driver and fairway woods.

Most sets of clubs are now available with steel or graphite shafts. There are two common misconceptions about graphite. Contrary to popular belief, you don't need to swing slower to time shots with a graphite shaft. And secondly, graphite shafts are not only of benefit to low-handicappers; a well fitted shaft can benefit players of any standard.

The equipment market will move over to graphite as golfers come to appreciate the added performance. Having invested in better shafts you must keep them in a 'graphite friendly' bag, with a fur or padded top which won't abrade the surface finish. This can be protected with a sock head cover or with tape wrapped around the shaft.

CHECKPOINTS

● The shaft flexes throughout the swing, but will lag slightly throughout your downswing, catching up just before impact.

● The best-timed swings will kick the shaft in momentarily before impact.

● Graphite shafts offer more scope for design and open up a greater range of possibilities when selecting clubs to suit.

1. Aldila's SpeedFit series of graphite shafts are designed, as the name suggests, to take the difficulty out of finding and fitting the correct shaft for your swing speed. Take great care when selecting any new shafts, it is important to get the right flex and torque for your swing.

The Set-Up

AIM AND GRIP

When playing any golf shot, you should start standing behind the ball, looking down the target line, visualizing the flight and the intended result. Having done this, move around to the ball, positioning the leading edge of your clubface at 90 degrees to the target line. Ignore the top edge, which changes from one iron club to another. Set the sole of the club almost flat on the ground but try to have the toe end fractionally raised.

Steady the club by holding the grip cap between your right thumb and index finger, ensuring the shaft is angled forwards a touch, your hands level with the ball or just ahead. Adopt a basic posture, tilting your spine angle forwards and pushing your bottom out. Now bring your left hand to the side of the club, fingers together and pointing at your toe line. Fold your hand around the club, palm and fingers together forming the grip. Lift the club up ahead of you, bending more at your wrist, and count two and a half knuckles in view, indicating 'neutral' – the position most likely to contribute to a square clubface at impact. Secondly, look for your thumb and index finger to be adjacent or 'stitched' together,

1. 'Neutral': left hand showing two and a half knuckles, palm of the right facing the target.

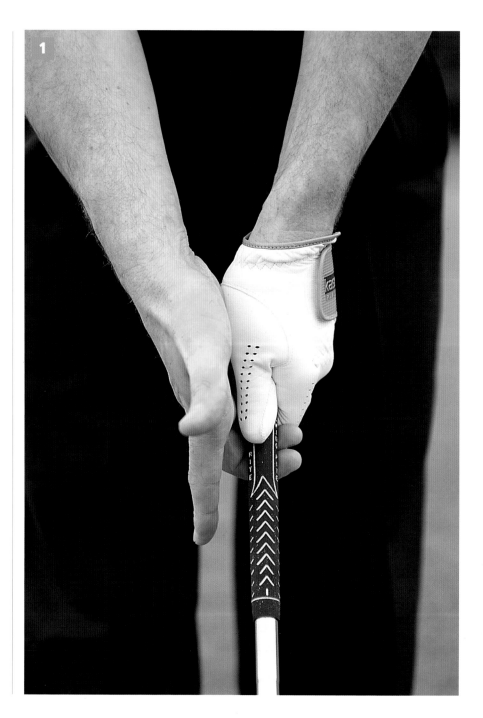

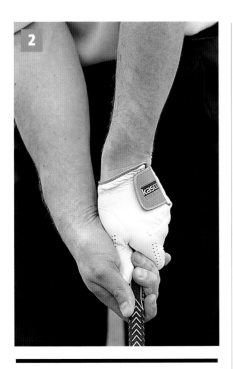

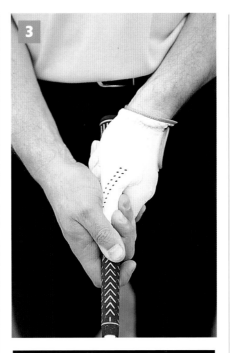

2. Incorrect. Both hands are positioned to the player's right of 'neutral'.

3. The left hand must show more knuckles, the palm of the right covering the gloved thumb.

4. The grip should sit under the fleshy part of the hand, held by left thumb and forefinger.

your thumb pushed up to sit compactly with the rest of the hand, not stretched down the grip. Develop a light grip, with any noticeable pressure in the upper three fingers. If your left hand is correctly positioned, you will be able to remove your thumb and index finger, still trapping the club underneath the fleshy part of your hand, while holding it in place with your fingers.

Now add your right hand. Its position is vital, so learn to set the hand correctly before adopting the overlap or interlock. Set your palm facing the target and keep it there. Then just ease your small finger over the index finger of the left, or slot it between the index and middle fingers to interlock. Fold the middle fingers of your right onto the club, keeping them together and butted up against the index finger of the left. Your right index finger forms a triggered position, separated from your middle finger. Finally, your thumb

should close over – the fleshy pad effectively locking the hand into position without applying any pressure.

The position of your hands on the club will influence the clubface position at impact. Pay particular attention to the knuckle count and the position of the right palm, which should face the target.

It matters little whether you overlap, interlock or place both hands fully on the club, so long as both hands work together in the swing. Separating your hands even slightly will force them to oppose one another, limiting clubhead speed and affecting clubface control.

Finally, grip pressure. Your grip must reflect the optimum tension required in your swing, which should be light if you are to turn freely and maximize clubhead speed. Tighten your grip and you will lock your body muscles, limiting your range of movement.

CHECKPOINTS

- Look from behind your target line and visualize the flight.

....

- Set the clubface down squarely to the target, the sole of the club fractionally raised at the toe.

....

- Position your left hand showing two and a half knuckles, thumb next to your index finger.

....

- Add your right hand, ensuring the palm faces the target.

....

- Keep your grip pressure light.

OVERLAP, INTERLOCKING OR BASEBALL?

It is essential that your grip achieves three points. Firstly, your hands must be positioned so that the clubface returns squarely at impact – they must be 'neutral' on the club. Secondly, you must find your optimum grip pressure. Your wrists must be able to hinge both back and through easily in order to transmit the power to the clubface, giving the distance. Lastly, your hands must always work together within the swing, rather than as separate units.

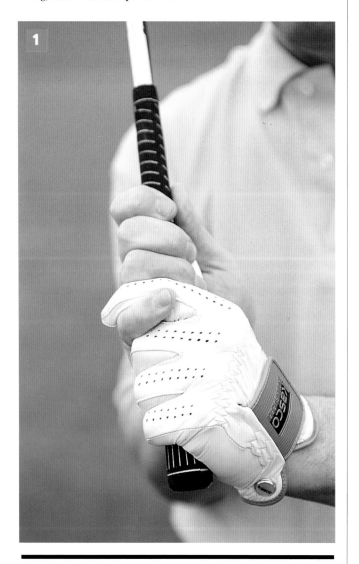

1. The popular 'interlocking' grip. It is important to use a shallow interlock, rather than jamming the fingers together.

The vast majority of tournament professionals use the overlapping, 'Vardon', grip. The small finger of your right hand should ride over the index finger of your left, usually finding the slot between that and your middle finger. Some find this awkward and prefer to let it rest over the index finger. In both cases the middle fingers of your right hand should be butted up against your left index finger.

A good grip reflects a compromise between power and control. If your hands are too far apart, you create more leverage in the swing, which is advantageous to clubhead speed. But if your hands fail to move together throughout, controlling the clubface position and transmitting clubhead speed to the ball, this will not translate into power for impact.

Many golfers prefer the interlocking grip. It offers a feeling of a more secure hold of the club. Your left index finger lifts off the shaft along with your right small finger, crossing over as you replace them. With your left hand on the club, add your right hand, palm opened out at first to ensure it faces the target. Now interlock, followed by folding your thumb over your left hand. The hand must be positioned as if overlapping, right palm facing the target. Many club golfers go wrong at this point. They interlock first – before establishing the position of their right hand – and jam their fingers together. The whole of each finger is crossed over with the other, but as you fold your hand over, it sits excessively right of neutral, too much underneath and in a 'strong' position. To the player, this grip feels more powerful as the club is held

CHECKPOINTS

● Your hands must be in a neutral position on the club, whatever grip you use.

● Use a shallow interlock, your fingers crossing at their middle joints.

● Don't interlock by jamming your fingers together as this positions your right hand incorrectly.

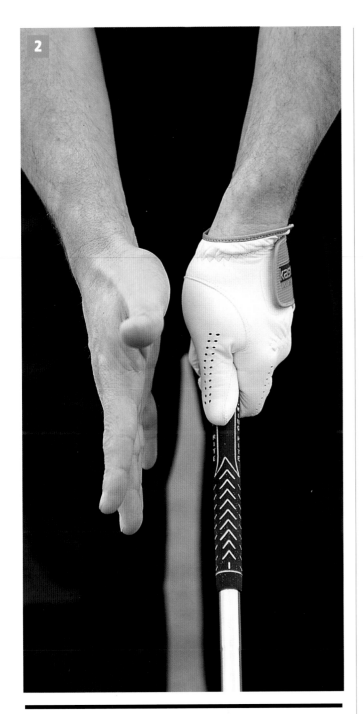

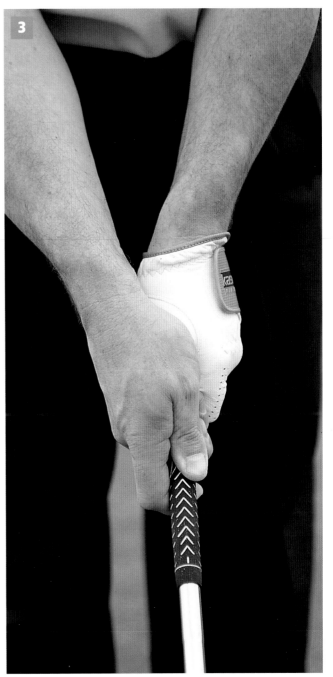

2. Add your right hand first, palm facing toward the target, whilst holding your hand to the side of the club.

3. Next, add the overlap or interlock, folding your hand over to cover your left thumb. Trigger your right forefinger.

more in the right palm, but is certain to have a marked effect on clubface control, and commonly results in hooking the ball to the left.

Lastly, the baseball grip. Highly recommended for juniors and less powerful players. If you want to maximize clubhead speed and can handle the possibility of less accurate shots, try this grip variation. Having positioned your left hand, butt the three upper fingers of your

right hand against the index finger of your left and fold the rest of your hand over. Still conceal your left thumb. This grip works better for golfers who slice as it promotes more action from your right hand and wrist, turning over through impact with more chance of squaring the face for impact. The slightly lower right hand position works more effectively, adding to the leverage within the swing.

GOLF BALL POSITIONING

Find an area on the practice ground where you can take practice swings and take divots. Adopt your normal address position, the clubhead starting off just left of centre in relation to your feet, weight evenly distributed. Swing at your normal speed and try to remove a shallow divot, 4 inches (10cm) long, at the base of the arc as part of a complete swing and full follow-through. The divot should start just left of centre in relation to the feet, and finish at the inside of the left heel. Position the golf ball at the point at which the club first hits the ground and you will strike solid shots, the ball will be collected by the clubface and a divot will be taken immediately after.

A routine at your set-up will help you position the golf ball at the optimum point. Aim your clubface squarely on the ball-to-target line. Grip the club and start with your feet together, a comfortable distance from the ball, knees slightly flexed. Open out your left foot 4 inches (10 cm), at the same time turning your toe out 10–15 degrees. Now open your right foot 8 inches (20 cm), again angling the toe outwards – this maximizes stability in the swing action. Of course, this will vary according to your swing type and preference, though not a great deal. With a little practice, you will develop a sound and repetitive routine for positioning the golf ball at your set-up.

The optimum position for the golf ball is fractionally before the lowest point in the swing arc, at a point where the swing direction coincides with the ball-to-target line and at the moment when the clubface is square. Complications arise when a golfer has to find a golf ball position which accommodates an open clubface and an outside-to-inside swing, typically standing further to the right so the ball appears opposite the left toe, so compensating for the error. The hooker of the ball moves the ball back in the stance to accomodate most successfully a swing direction from inside-to-outside, with the clubface closed.

To achieve consistency, every swing you make should be fundamentally the same. Assuming an orthodox swing technique, this logically means there is one base to the swing arc, always falling left of centre, always around 4 inches (10 cm) inside the left heel. It should stay there for every club, from the wedge to the driver. Simply widen your right foot for the bigger swings and narrow it for more lofted irons.

1. The ball must be positioned just before the lowest point in the swing arc. This enables the ball to be cleanly struck and a shallow divot to be taken.

Many golfers choose to move the ball positioning according to the club being played – further back in the stance for shorter irons to 'hit down more', theoretically creating additional backspin; opposite the left toe for the driver to hit with an ascending blow. This is perfectly workable for the skilled golfer and is used by some of the world's most successful players. However, it creates too many variables for the

2. A common error. The ball is positioned forward of the ideal position, which will result in striking the turf before the ball.

3. Ideally the ball should be positioned just left of centre. It is at this point that the swing is most likely to coincide with the ball to target line.

average or unskilled player. Playing the ball from further forward in the stance for tee shots encourages a sliding of the lower body, your hips and legs having to drive left to allow the clubhead to meet the back of the ball. A downswing sequence incorporating such a forceful lower body action requires a high degree of coordination and athleticism, and is therefore beyond most players.

CHECKPOINTS

● Take practice swings to establish the lowest point in your swing arc.

....

● The base of the arc should fall left of centre, the divot ending opposite your left heel.

....

● Use the set-up routine of stepping off your feet.

....

● Keep the ball position constant, always the same distance inside your left heel.

DISTANCE FROM THE BALL

Establishing the correct distance from the ball is a major concern for all golfers, especially those relatively new to the game who are trying to determine this for the range of shaft lengths. Assuming your clubs are standard length, you must accommodate a driver at 42 inches (1.07 m) as well as the sand iron measuring 35 inches (89 cm), and everything in between. Good players instinctively know how far away to stand, though feeling comfortable varies from day to day. The shaft length obviously dictates the distance, so start by placing the clubhead down behind the ball with the shaft angled as the club design suggests, then position your feet.

Some golfers like to drop the shaft of the club onto their knee, or a point above it, to check that the end of the club is just above the

1. One way of finding the correct distance to stand from the ball is to stand upright and hold your arms ahead of you, letting your elbows lightly brush the sides of you chest.

2. Your upper arms should be positioned so they touch your sides with no visible gap.

left knee. This can be a reliable method of establishing a good distance from the ball, and does at least ensure some consistency, but it is not recommended as you have to move out of posture to make the check.

Try another approach to finding your distance. This works with every iron and wood in your set, but start with a medium iron. Stand upright, knees just a touch flexed, your weight evenly spread between toes and

3. The correct distance from the ball must be established at your set-up. If you have located your ideal position, you will find that as you swing back and through, you will be able to turn freely and swing fully. From the correct position the ball will be collected as you swing through. There should be no attempt to manipulate or steer the clubhead to force it into the correct path, as occurs when a position too near or at an excessive distance from the ball is adopted.

heels. Hold your hands in front of you, just below chest height, wrists angled, shaft angled upwards until the head is face high in front of you. The insides of your upper arms should very lightly brush the sides of your chest. Now simply tilt your upper body forwards, your shoulders dropping more over the ball, your lower back pushed out by the hips, knees bending a touch more to maintain the weight evenly between toes and heels. The clubhead finds the optimum distance from the ball – the distance most likely to produce solid shots. Practise this until you recognize the sensation of this set-up. As the shaft length increases for the longer irons and woods, the shaft will fall further from you, but still encourage a taller spine angle, body less angled over the ball. This agrees with the set-up and swing required for these clubs, dictating a wider swing arc and flatter plane. The common factor is the connection between arms and body.

Your height and build influence your posture. Shorter, stocky golfers will stand further away, creating room to move their arms and club down and into a completed follow-through. Taller golfers will stand closer, their hands falling closer to their left thigh. This dictates a more upright plane which is more suitable for them.

Your swing style may additionally influence your distance from the ball. Taller golfers will probably swing more from their arms with an up and down action, the slightly closer ball being most suitable. Shorter golfers are likely to swing on a flatter plane using more of a body action; this will throw the clubhead away from them in the downswing and requires the ball to be further away.

CHECKPOINTS

● The key variable is the length of the shaft. Stand closer when putting and chipping, stand further away for driving and longer irons.

● Some golfers like to drop their left hand onto their left leg to confirm a good distance away.

● The best method of finding the optimum distance is to stand upright first, angling your body forwards until your upper arms rest gently against your chest, then bending your knees.

BODY ALIGNMENT AND POSTURE

Body alignment and posture are formed together at the address position. With poor alignment, the direction of ball flight will be inconsistent. If you have poor body posture, the ball strike will be variable with distance always a problem.

When forming your address position, establish a logically correct body alignment which should be practised initially with a medium iron. A square stance is mostly determined by the clubface aim and shoulder alignment, and if these two are correct, the hips, legs and arms tend to follow naturally. The common error is to concern yourself exclusively with the line of your toes whilst forgetting your upper body alignment.

Assess every shot from behind the ball-to-target line, then aim the clubface down that line – or squarely. This is the best guide to shoulder alignment, as the body will automatically follow clubface aim.

On the practice ground, you should constantly check and re-check your aim and alignment by playing towards a specific target, and ask a friend to line your shoulders up squarely. Remember that the shoulders must not be pointing at the flagstick, but will appear more to the left of the target when aligned squarely. The shoulders will feel tilted at the address position, enhancing that feeling of the left shoulder being partly in view when looking to the target side.

Posture in a golf swing is related to the distance you stand from the golf ball. The correct distance from the ball with good body posture will control the weight distribution between heels and toes, giving a base to the swing action.

Good posture will allow you enough room to swing the club through impact without any restriction, and without having to reach out for the ball. The correct distance, posture and weight distribution will be pre-set at the address; at impact these should each be returned to the same positions.

The spine angle at the address position is critical, as the upper body angles forward from the hips, and the legs respond by flexing slightly. A good posture will push your backside out, encouraging two positive angles in your body posture, one formed as the spine angle tilts forward from the hips, the second as the knees flex slightly. Your upper body

1. Excellent posture. Knees flexed but not bent and the upper body is angled forwards with the arms hanging down from the shoulders without tension.

(including your head) is now set at one constant angle, best explained as the spine angle. The swing should maintain this angle, returning the club at impact with the angle constant. Poor body posture will force you to adjust mid-swing to accommodate the arm swing. Adjustments during the swing prevent the development of a repetitive action.

Your upper body should feel tall – use your height and keep your body in the best position from which to pivot. Your arms must hang freely from the shoulders, forming an angle between them and the club shaft. If the arms are held too high, the spine angle will be too upright. Don't allow your chin to drop down against the chest. You must try to ignore everything you've ever learned about keeping your head down, as it is essential that your swing has freedom of movement. All good swings have this freedom, and a sound posture is the key to it.

3. Poor posture. The hands are positioned too low, pulling the upper body over the ball too much.

2. Check your body alignment by placing the shaft of a golf club along your shoulder line.

CHECKPOINTS

● Good body alignment starts with a square clubface at the address position. Your shoulders will follow what the clubface dictates.

● Your shoulder alignment is most important, followed by your hips, legs and feet.

● Remember the feeling of good body alignment, your left shoulder noticeably higher than your right.

● A good body posture is dependent upon a good distance from the ball.

● Set two positive angles at the address position, one being the spine angle, the other the slight flex of the knees.

Swing Concepts

THE UPPER BODY PIVOT

The upper body pivot is the turning of the body around the spine during the golf swing. It is one of the most important parts of the swing and contributes much to the swing shape. Isolate it by positioning a club behind your shoulders, hands holding it in place on either side. Adopt your normal posture, spine tilted forwards, knees a touch flexed, weight evenly spread between toes and heels, toes angled out around 15 degrees. Now turn your shoulders with no hint of dipping the left shoulder. Feel your left knee working towards the ball or pointing just behind it, whilst your right knee maintains at least some flexibility. Try to achieve a 90-degree turn going back, left shoulder arriving under and in front of your chin, your back facing the target. Check in a mirror. Your shoulders should have turned at 90 degrees to your inclined spine angle.

This is a potentially powerful top of the backswing position. Your shoulders have turned, your hips have partially resisted the turn, your legs more so. The right leg, remaining flexed throughout, has stretched the muscles across the left side of your back, coiling them to build and store energy. Your left leg, moving more at the ball but not sagging across to the right side, further resists the turn.

Now reverse this move, starting with the left knee working towards the target, opening the gap between your knees whilst your hips respond by starting to turn. Both knees will rotate together at this point, hips and shoulders unwinding as a consequence. Now feel your right shoulder turning through, working underneath and around your chin, staying low to maintain that critical spine angle. Release your right heel and fully shift the weight, finishing up using the toe as nothing more than a balance point, with your right heel fully up.

There are three stages to the most efficient pivot. Backswing turn, start of the downswing as the body finds its ideal position to square the clubface for impact, followed by the right side moving through to the

1. Turn fully going back, your left shoulder working into a position underneath the chin. The shaft of the club is now at 90 degrees to the spine angle.

swing's completion. These stages join in one complete action – back and through, with no obvious pause. As you practise this drill, try to mirror each position, left shoulder down going back, right shoulder replacing it. Be aware of this sensation, as it confirms the spine angle has stayed constant, with your upper body simply rotating around it.

An important point to grasp is that having set your body posture – with particular emphasis placed on the spine angle – you must maintain this until the ball is in flight, most clearly identified as three-quarters through, arms around shoulder height. At this point in the swing, your right side will be forced to lift.

Also the rotational nature of the pivot incorporates a weight shift to your right side going back and to your left side as you reverse the swing. Don't try to keep your head still, but instead feel your upper body shifting behind the ball going back, feeling as though you are centred over your right hip at the top. By the end of the swing, you should have your body centred over your left hip.

CHECKPOINTS

● Isolate the pivot by positioning a club behind your shoulders.

● Turn back and through, working your left shoulder down going back, replacing it with your right shoulder past impact.

● Turn your shoulders and resist this turn with your legs.

● Incorporate a weight shift in your pivot, turning over your hip each side of the swing.

2. Turn through to face the target, but make sure that your right shoulder remains lower than your left – in this way the backswing pivot is mirrored.

3. A common error. The player's right shoulder has lifted and as a result his spine angle has changed. Swings finishing in this position are likely to top or thinly strike the ball.

FEET AND LEGS

The function of the feet and legs in the swing is to support the upper body pivot. Your legs provide stability for the swing action, whilst accommodating a full shoulder turn in the backswing and follow-through. In addition, there must be weight transference to your right side in the backswing and to the target-side in the downswing and follow-through.

Start at the address position. Set yourself up with a medium iron and the ball positioned one clubhead inside the left heel and your weight spread evenly between left and right feet. Sense a springiness in your knees and keep them just slightly bent, with your hips pushed back to create the space to swing your arms. Feel tall at the set-up, spine angle tilted forwards but your head away from your chest. Position your feet so that your toes point outwards some 10–15 degrees. Keep your heels roughly shoulders' width apart.

As your shoulders turn in the backswing, your feet and legs must contain the turn. Your shoulders should turn 90 degrees whilst your left heel remains on the ground or very close to it. Early into your backswing – arms and shaft not yet horizontal – you should sense the weight has moved more towards your right side. This movement is mostly lateral, the weight actually transferring across, the shoulder turn dictating a slight rotational shift of weight towards your right heel. From here to the completion of the backswing, the shoulder turn dictates, so the weight shift is purely rotational. During your backswing, sense how the weight moves

progressively towards your right heel, until at the top your toes can move. The weight shift is limited by your right leg, which should remain flexed throughout the swing, gradually straightening but retaining some bend at the knee. Your left knee should bend more than the right, pointing directly at the ball at the top of your backswing.

You can now judge the importance of having your toes pointing outwards at the set-up. The right leg must accommodate not only a 90-degree shoulder turn but a 45-degree hip turn, which places stress on the knee joint if the right foot is at right angles to the target line. Angle the right toe out, feel the flexibility of the knee at your address position and try to

hold this at the completion of the backswing. Feel as though your upper body is supported by your right hip and leg at the top.

Starting down is most important, your knees opening up more of a gap as you assume a slightly squatter position, left knee working towards the target as the change of swing direction commences. This pulls the weight away from your right heel and more centrally between the feet as the club arrives at halfway down, shaft parallel to the ground. You now have the perfect position for the clubhead to be delivered into the back of the ball, the upper body fully supported by the legs, weight evenly spread, both knees flexed.

Through impact and beyond, your legs must continue to accommodate the turning action of your shoulders and hips, but the acceleration of the clubhead past the hitting area pulls your right side through. You do not 'kick' your right knee across – it is pulled across and the heel pulled up by your body turn. Try to complete your swing with your hips fully facing the target. Your left leg should be braced, knee locked back as the weight shifts to the heel.

1. The legs and feet must support the upper body pivot, with the left knee pointing towards the ball at the top of the backswing, while the right knee retains some flexibility.

2. It is important to hold the right knee flex going back in order to resist the upper body turn.

3. The turning motion of your hips and shoulders in the downswing and follow-through will pull your right knee and heel through. Try to finish the shot with your hips facing the target.

CHECKPOINTS

● Feel the weight evenly spread at your set-up.
....

● Start back with a feeling of shifting your weight, left leg bending more at the ball.
....

● Maintain some flex in your right leg at the top.
....

● Start down by feeling squat, left knee working towards the target.
....

● Finish on your left side, right toe assisting the balance.

CENTRIFUGAL FORCE

A golf swing need not become a study in physics and mechanical force, but there is one aspect of physics that greatly influences the completed swing. Centrifugal force is the outward pulling of a weighted object from a centre. In the golf swing, the mass of the arms, hands and clubhead pull away from the swing centre in response to the pivot.

Take an example of swinging a child around you. As you turn to provide the motion, the child becomes far lighter and very little energy is required to maintain the orbit. Centrifugal force, pulling outwards, reduces the force of gravity downwards. The same concept applies to the golf swing – principally to the downswing at speed. The upper body turn, or pivot, creates the circular motion whilst the arms, hands and clubhead respond to this by swinging freely down, through impact and up again for the follow-through. The orbit is constant and requires little or no physical application itself.

1. Practise hitting shots with your feet together to develop a free-swinging action.

2. Everyone swings freely when the plane of the swing is flatter – as in the baseball swing.

Centrifugal force can benefit your golf swing, because it dictates that the clubhead follow a constant orbit or path as it approaches impact. It assists greatly in generating clubhead speed without the need for physical strength, and pulls the arms and wrists downwards through impact to ensure that the ball is solidly struck.

The pivot – upper body turn – is the key to harnessing and maximizing centrifugal force. The swing originates in the lower to middle back. Set your spine angle at the address position; it must now remain constant throughout your backswing, downswing and past impact until the ball is well on its way. Any change to this most vital of angles will disrupt centrifugal force and affect clubhead speed. Remain at a constant angle, and the force is transmitted via your arms and hands to maximize clubhead speed.

If harnessed properly, centrifugal force can benefit all golfers, but it is particularly useful for young and women players.

To maximize the benefits of centrifugal force, ensure that both your grip pressure and your overall muscle tension are light. A successful golf swing requires freedom that is inhibited by applying a vise-like grip and freezing your body into a static, locked position even before it starts back.

Take plenty of practice swings and sense the clubhead moving in an arc around the body. Do not manipulate this, but instead permit it to find its own path – that dictated by the correct pivoting of the upper body. Your swing must be fairly complete, so encourage the shoulders to turn fully 90 degrees in the backswing and 120 degrees for the follow-through, providing your individual

3. A free-swinging action down and through impact maximizes centrifugal force and adds to clubhead speed. This results in longer shots, irrespective of body strength, helping weaker players in particular.

flexibility permits. Allow the sole of the clubhead to brush the grass away through the impact area, removing a small, shallow divot. Centrifugal force is maximized when you gently accelerate your clubhead speed throughout the downswing and encourage the follow-through to be complete. The backswing will be relatively slow and the downswing twice as fast.

CHECKPOINTS

● Posture and pivot are vital to maximizing centrifugal force.

● Turn back and through maintaining your spine angle.

● Apply a light grip pressure and swing freely.

● Gently accelerate through your downswing in order to maximize clubhead speed.

WEIGHT DISTRIBUTION

Body weight must transfer in the direction that you are swinging the club. Your upper body must move freely both swinging back and through, thereby creating the necessary weight transference. Good weight transference is rotational. At your address position with a medium iron, your weight should be evenly distributed between heels and toes, and your left and right sides. This provides you with stability and balance. With the driver from the tee, you should encourage a slightly ascending strike by starting off with the weight favouring your right side. With the shorter, more lofted irons you can encourage a more descending strike by pre-setting the weight 60% on your left side and 40% to your right.

Even before the shaft has reached horizontal in the backswing, your weight will have shifted noticeably to your right side. As the backswing progresses, the weight continues to move across, but as a rotational weight transfer. As the club swings upwards in the second half of your backswing, the weight is felt mostly through your right heel. At the top of your backswing, your shoulders should have turned fully 90 degrees, the hips 45 degrees and the knees will have reacted, the left bending towards the golf ball, the right straightening but remaining slightly flexed. You won't be centred any longer, as you were at the address position. The turn of the body and weight transfer will position your right hip over your right leg, shifting the upper body behind the ball.

In the downswing many golfers move to their left side too early, shifting the upper body and head forwards of the ball at impact. There must be a transition, a change of direction early into the downswing which will

1. Your weight must not remain central. It should shift noticeably to your right side going back. The weight will be felt mostly through the right heel.

2. Early into the downswing your weight will transfer from your right to your left side. Your right knee should pull across causing the heel to become raised.

3. A very common error. The weight has not moved fully to the golfer's left side during the downswing and the right heel remains planted to the ground.

4

CHECKPOINTS

● Your weight must move in the direction that you are swinging the club for maximum power.

....

● Don't try to keep your head still, as this inhibits the natural tendency to move weight as you swing.

....

● Weight transference is rotational, moving into your right heel through your backswing.

....

● Feel the weight shift to your left side as you swing down and through, finishing with most on your left heel.

....

● Your right knee and heel are pulled through in response to this weight shift.

4. A well-balanced follow-through with the body angles retained. The weight has been fully transferred to the left side, felt mostly in the heel as the leg gradually straightens at the completion of the swing. Try to hold this position until the ball has landed.

position the body, arms, wrists and club ready for impact. You don't move to your left side, but rather centralize the weight distribution as the left arm pulls downwards. You will notice that the left knee is opening up, separating away from the right as the hips begin to rotate and promote the correct downswing shape.

The objective at impact is to have the weight on the left side, with the left hip positioned so that it pulls the right leg through, bending at the knee and gradually raising the heel. There is no independent kick of this knee; instead it responds to the hip action. Your left hip will turn to your left side and, the more it does this, the greater the tendency to straighten that leg. This forms a lower body support for the upper body forward swing and follow-through.

At the completion of the swing, the shaft of the club should finish in a position behind your neck, your shoulders having now turned through 120 degrees and your hips fully facing in the direction of the target. Your left leg should now be supporting your upper body weight, while your right heel will be raised with your right toe maintaining contact with the ground to ensure balance.

TIMING

Timing refers to the sequence of swing movements or positions. The expression is usually reserved for the downswing sequence as this has the greatest influence over the quality of impact and the resulting ball flight. A well-timed swing, combining all stages of the sequence smoothly, will return the clubhead squarely and powerfully at impact, lightly brushing the ground with an iron club and just missing the ground with the driver from a tee.

The downswing can be broken down into three stages, each a separate movement initially but, as they blend in the completed swing, they combine to deliver the maximum clubhead speed with a relatively small effort. The first stage will feel as though your left arm is moving downwards whilst your legs and hips begin to rotate. The shoulders are relatively passive whilst the arm swing is more positive. This will preserve the angle of the wrists, which will remain unchanged from the top of the backswing position. Continue this until the shaft is in a horizontal position, where it should also be parallel to the ball-to-target line. The shoulders will be partially turned away from the target, perhaps 10 to 20 degrees from square. The hips now face the ball with your weight evenly distributed.

The second part of the downswing moves the club through impact to the corresponding position on the other side, the shaft mirroring its downswing position. The right heel will have left the ground, the shoulders now turned some 50–60 degrees, the hips about the same.

The completion of the swing moves the arms upwards until the wrists hinge and the club shaft is encouraged to finish behind your neck. After some practice with this sequence of three stages to the downswing, you can blend parts two and three together to leave a two-part downswing. Eventually this becomes one complete action.

1. At the start of the downswing your shoulders should be relatively passive, while your arm swing is more positive.

2. An example of poor timing. The wrists are ahead of the ball which will result in an open clubface at impact.

3. If the shot is well timed, your right shoulder will remain low throughout impact and beyond.

4. The dominant right shoulder has dictated this faulty downswing, which has finished too high.

Poor timing can have many results, the most common being the shot that flies weakly to the right of target. Many golfers unwind with the shoulders too quickly, forcing the arms to move away from the body. At impact the shaft tends to be angled excessively forwards which in turn leaves the clubface in a slightly open position. The contact will feel less than solid, especially with woods and longer irons, the shot frequently struck from the heel. This is the drive that leaves you more than your usual distance from the flag, making longer holes especially difficult or unreachable with the second shot.

Poor timing can also result from the wrists and upper body being fractionally before the clubhead. The clubface is allowed to overtake as the wrists collapse just prior to impact. This is usually associated with novice golfers who have not learned to turn their shoulders in the backswing. Not only will these shots tend to be weak, but there is also a tendency to strike the ground before the ball or to thin the shot.

CHECKPOINTS

● At impact your arms, wrists and club return to the same position as at the set-up, your body turning more left.

....

● The start of your downswing is where timing is critical.

....

● Feel as though your right shoulder stays back momentarily to encourage your arms to start down to the inside path.

....

● Hold the right shoulder back until your arms have rotated through impact, squaring the clubface.

RHYTHM AND TEMPO

Rhythm describes the smoothness in the swing motion. A rhythmical swing blends each movement to create a single complete action. There are several reasons why this is important. Firstly, a smooth swing motion assists in maximizing clubhead speed for impact. Secondly, the key to distance is to use your body muscles efficiently, swinging the club freely from your arms whilst turning back and through with your shoulders. Thirdly, a swing with rhythm will have a smooth transition from the backswing's completion to early into your downswing, avoiding a major problem area for many golfers who use their right side too early. This error causes the shoulders to unwind prematurely, throwing the club into an outside-to-inside path and pulling the ball straight left or slicing to the right.

Try a simple exercise. Address the ball with your feet together, initially using a 6-iron. Turn freely and swing back and through fully. Work at maintaining balance and control. Feel the clubhead swing freely and use the swinging action to produce the distance, which should be near 90% of your normal distance with this club.

1. Swinging two clubs together can help to improve the rhythm of your swing.

2. Keep your grip pressure light to prevent muscle tension.

CHECKPOINTS

- ● Try hitting shots with your feet together.

....

- ● A rhythmical swing will have both control and a freedom of movement.

....

- ● 'Swing slowly': the standard advice of 'swing slowly' can limit clubhead speed.

....

- ● Set your tempo in the pre-swing waggle to mirror the swing to follow.

More identifiable, and certainly more influential on your golf shots, is tempo, the pace of your swing. Observation of top players proves that tempo is individual, with both slow and very fast swings capable of hitting consistently good shots – so long as the sequence of movements (timing) is correct. You have to find a workable tempo for your individual swing, which you may find will match your nature.

One of the greatest myths in golf is that you should 'swing slowly'. Adherence to this causes so many golfers – most commonly women – to struggle generating clubhead speed. The swing must be brisk enough to build sufficient power to drive the ball forwards and into the air. A fast swing is not necessarily a poor swing, providing that the movements are in correct sequence.

Too fast a backswing will throw the club into an overswing and produce a loss of control; it will also affect the recovery of the club as the downswing starts. The most likely

3. Make sure that the transition from downswing to backswing is seamless and smooth.

first move down will be dominated by the right shoulder; this will throw the body into the shot excessively.

Avoid the deliberate swing acceleration: slow back followed by a rush to the ball. This disrupts the vital change of direction as the

downswing starts, again tending to cause the right side to unwind prematurely.

The only way to find a workable tempo is to experiment on the practice ground. Try out a range of both slower and faster swings, monitoring the results.

CLUBHEAD LAG AND RELEASE

In the completed swing, the downswing sequence is not a simple reversal of the backswing. Instead, you must develop a sequence that controls impact and produces the 'hit' when required.

At the top of your backswing, you should have an angle formed at your right wrist. It folds back on itself and feels as though the palm is underneath the shaft. Your right elbow must be tucked in, remaining fairly close to your left arm rather than separating outwards. As your downswing begins, retain the right hand angle. Try to drop the shaft to the inside path, effectively looping it a touch behind you as part of the sequence. Your hips and legs dictate the body action, leaving your shoulders behind as they turn gradually to face the golf ball. Your shoulders and arms must not move together to initiate the downswing. As the shaft nears horizontal,

your right elbow will work more tightly to your body than in the backswing. You have now delayed the release until the precise moment it is required. Do not confuse this with the so-called 'late hit'. By holding the right wrist angle for longer, then encouraging the right hand, lower arm and shoulder to unfold in the most effective order you are lagging the club and not delaying the release.

Develop this sequence during your practice sessions. Set the angle of the right wrist, and keep this constant until the shaft reaches halfway down, and then feel your right side turning through. Combine this with the feeling of looping your downswing

initially to the inside path, thus keeping your shoulders out of the action until they catch up and eventually overtake past impact.

THE RELEASE 'Release' describes the way in which the hands, wrists and lower arms combine to return the clubface to the back of the ball at speed. This area of the swing is critical to the ball's flight, because you will either capitalize on all the preceding swing movements, or destroy all the good that went before. The problem is that the movement occurs very quickly, so you could be excused for being unsure quite what has happened. Watch your ball flight for clues.

A well-timed release action will return the club to the position it was in at address. The dynamic action of swinging the club will position your hips and shoulders left of target at impact, weight mostly on your target side leg. The shaft must return to its vertical or slightly angled forwards position, the clubface should be square to the intended target and the sole of the club must be flat to the ground.

Review your technique, starting halfway down with the shaft horizontal: your right side provides the hit, wrist angle flattening as your lower arms rotate, so squaring the clubface for impact. The downward uncocking of the wrists ensures the sole of the club brushes the ground just past impact, ideally taking a shallow divot with the irons.

If the release is delayed or too slow, the clubface will be left open at impact, slicing the ball to the right. An extreme of this will top and thin shots as the sole of the clubhead fails to find the back of the ball. Too early a release will roll the clubface closed for impact, hooking the ball away to the left side.

1. Maintain the angle of your wrists until they are at waist height in the downswing.

2. Make sure that you use your right side through impact; feel your arms 'rotate' to enable the clubface to square up for impact.

3. Your right arm must become extended once your swing has passed the point of impact. Point your right thumb up and direct the palm behind you.

4. Use this practice drill to help promote the all-important release action. Place your right hand well below your left to encourage arm rotation.

CHECKPOINTS

● Think of the club lagging in the downswing.

● Hold the angle formed at your right wrist until halfway down.

● Feel your club loop a little to the inside path to hold back your right side.

● Feel your right wrist unfold, gradually straightening as your arm starts to rotate.

CONTROLLING BACKSWING LENGTH

There is no single, optimum length to a backswing, as is confirmed by watching tournament professionals, some of whom use noticeably long or short swings, but still produce the necessary control, power and repetition required.

The average golfer would do best to adhere to an orthodox technique, limiting the backswing length to around the horizontal position with the longest clubs, stopping short of this with more lofted irons. The longer the backswing, the more potential clubhead speed, but only if you can recover the control early in your downswing, and you possess the flexibility and hand/eye co-ordination necessary to find the back of the ball each time. In theory, a very short swing is likely to restrict clubhead speed, but it is also likely to be of benefit to you in returning the clubface solidly at impact.

There are three critical areas of your swing which you must address in order to find your ideal backswing.

WRISTS AND HANDS At the top of the backswing, the left arm is extended, the hands and wrists hinge, but still retain control over the club. Poor control at this point, leading to the club shaft collapsing into an overswing, is usually caused by a poor grip at the address position. Your hands should be positioned underneath the club shaft at the top, thumbs supporting the weight of the club. Too lazy a grip will allow the club to be loose in the left

1. The left wrist has collapsed. The downswing will be difficult to recover and control, and it is unlikely that distance will be maximized.

2. From the correct position, the angle of the wrist is more controllable whilst the right supports the shaft. A shorter backswing than in pic 1 but with greater potential for distance.

CHECKPOINTS

● The optimum position at the backswing's completion should turn your shoulders 90 degrees.

● Your shaft should reach horizontal, stopping before this with shorter, more lofted clubs.

● Control the amount of wrist hinge, feeling your thumbs locating under the shaft to support the club.

● Maintain left arm extension throughout your backswing to preserve swing radius.

● Control your lower body action, particularly your right knee, which should retain some flexibility.

3. Practise your top of the backswing position by reversing the sequence of arm swing and wrist hinge. Lift your arms up slightly but cock your wrists until the clubhead is in a position just above head height as shown. Now simply add your backswing pivot and feel the shaft of the golf club locate just over your right shoulder.

hand, causing the butt end to move away from the palm of the hand. More importantly, too tight a grip at the address position can cause the club to be jerked away from the ball. To correct this error, maintain a constantly firm and light grip pressure throughout.

LEFT ARM The left arm sets the swing radius in the backswing. It is important that it remains extended, and doesn't fold or bend. Your left arm must not be absolutely straight, as this leads to excessive swing tension, but if it folds, the club will pass its controlled position into an overswing. Left arm collapse is usually linked to an incomplete shoulder turn. Poor upper body action prevents the left arm from extending to retain control, and the arm folds as a result. To correct this, concentrate on achieving a complete shoulder turn, to at least 80 degrees, and extend the left arm to a constant radius throughout the backswing.

LOWER BODY At the top of the backswing, the shoulders will have turned through around 90 degrees. The lower body will obviously respond to this, the hips turning around half the amount the shoulders turn. It is important to make sure that your legs resist your upper shoulder and hip turn, so that the first movement of the downswing is a reflex action rather than a conscious change of swing direction. Use the right leg to 'support' the backswing body turn, and retain control by maintaining some flexibility even at the completion of your backswing. If your lower body collapses, the weight will move to the outside of the right leg at the top, and the hips and shoulders over-rotate, thereby losing power as you fight – in most cases unsuccessfully – to regain control in the downswing. Try to maintain right knee flex throughout the swing, and turn your shoulders while resisting with the lower body.

The Model Swing

THE MODEL GOLF SWING

iven that the 'perfect swing' does not exist – a fact evidenced by the variety of swing techniques used by top players – there is no definitive swing to copy. It is possible to learn from watching top players, as each has points that merit imitation, but don't try and duplicate a swing wholesale, as you are an individual and no two swings can be identical. However, successful swings exhibit certain characteristics and, to this extent, there is a 'model swing' that you can work towards.

The easiest way to learn, improve or check a golf swing is to break it down into small, manageable sections. Once you have learned to recognize how each swing position looks and feels, link them together to build clubhead speed within a controlled, repeatable action.

Ideally, everyone should learn a model swing from day one, guided by a skilled teaching professional. With just one set of good swing positions grooved into place, improvement follows easily. However, most start golf in a less formal way, and swings tend to evolve over a

1. Correct. Your arms move first in the downswing.

2. Practise your lower body turn by holding a shaft against your hips.

period of time, the player picking up a tip here or making an adjustment there. The end product can be every bit as orthodox and effective, but it leaves far too much to chance.

The model swing will inevitably look orthodox. Everyone should strive to swing the club in a similar way, but your swing will evolve over time as you find certain wayward shots affect your scores. If you tend to hook because your hands and lower arms rotate excessively just prior to impact, you will have to develop an action resisting this. You could work at turning your hips more to create space for your arms to swing through. You will need to identify a backswing length most suitable for your ability level, flexibility and preference. Too many golfers swing too far back, particularly during the early stages of learning. Whilst a longer backswing has the potential for more distance, control and repetition must be part of the formula. If not, the odd shot flies long and straight, but the remainder are hit left and right or mishit. Younger players can easily turn fully, achieving a backswing pivot in excess of 90 degrees. Most senior golfers have less flexibility and, therefore, have to limit backswing length accordingly. This distance loss should be compensated for by becoming more accurate, more consistent or simply improving the short game.

Use the model swing as a basis for your technique. Identify the key points at stationary positions, then link them together to produce one complete action. The model swing is broken down into segments over the following pages.

CHECKPOINTS

● The easiest way to learn or improve is to break the swing technique down into stationary positions.

....

● Check each stage and link them together once you can 'feel' the movement required.

....

● Once it is learned, you may have to adapt the swing until it fits your build, strength and degree of flexibility.

....

● Experiment with mild variations on the model swing to find what works best for you, but don't deviate from the orthodox.

3. Use this drill to practise the all important backswing pivot. Since it requires no clubs this drill can be used anywhere. Position your hands across the front of your shoulders, crossing them over against your chest. Don't forget to adopt a good golfing posture, bending at your hips to angle your spine forwards. Flex your knees a touch and ensure your weight is evenly distributed between left and right, toes and heels. Make sure your chin stays up and away from your chest. Now simply turn to your right side as if making a backswing, ensuring your left shoulder is angled downwards a touch. Your lower body will respond to your upper body turn, but try to resist, keeping your left heel on the ground and maintaining some flexibility at your right knee. Turn back to face the ball and continue to the mirrored position on the other side, keeping a low right shoulder while, this time, encouraging your right knee to move through to meet the left. Try to finish with your right heel fully raised from the floor.

ADDRESS POSITION

SIDE ON Aim the clubface squarely to the target line, then align the body parallel to this with particular emphasis on the position of the shoulders and hips. Set the correct golfing posture, angling the upper body forwards, bending at the hips to encourage your bottom to push out, creating the necessary clearance for the arms to swing freely down and through. Flex the knees slightly, but use your legs to maintain balance and support the upper body pivot. Feel your weight evenly spread between the toes and the heels. Keep your chin up and away from your chest. Your arms should be hanging down from the shoulders, with your right elbow fractionally folded towards the side.

FACE ON The clubface is square to the target line, ball positioned 4 inches (10cm) inside the left heel. Feet are roughly shoulders' width apart to give stability during the swing, though not so wide that they restrict the pivot. The shaft is vertical, pointing at the centre of the stomach. The hands are positioned as they should return for impact, left hand showing two and a half knuckles, palm of the right facing the target. The right shoulder is lower than the left because the right hand is lower on the club. The head is positioned a touch behind the ball. Keep the grip pressure and overall body tension light.

1. A clear example of a poor address position. The player is standing too far away from the ball, causing his upper body to be positioned over the ball. His weight is also too far towards the toes.

2. The correct address position. The upper body is angled forwards at the hips, chin up and well away from the chest. The arms are in a good position and the knees are flexed a touch to give the optimum stability for the swing that is about to take place.

3. Poor upper body alignment. The player's shoulders are aiming well left of the intended target. This will influence the swing shape and make it impossible to move the clubhead through impact on the ideal path.

4. A good set-up. The ball is positioned just left of centre, the shaft is angled forwards a touch. The right shoulder is just lower than the left, inclining the head to the side. Weight is evenly distributed.

STARTING BACK

FACE ON The first movement is a co-ordinated swing of the arms and a pivot of the upper body until the shaft reaches 8 o'clock when viewed from face on. The initial movement going back should be smooth. Start back by turning the right shoulder away, hip responding a touch. The arms and club move away in a co-ordinated action, sweeping the clubhead back on a wide, shallow and gradual arc around the body. The emphasis is on a turning of the upper body, with no lateral slide. Feel the left shoulder starting to turn and incline downwards. Already the whole body is pivoting, the shoulders are around 30 degrees turned and the hips half

this. The arms must remain in co-ordination. The right elbow begins to fold away towards your right side whilst the left remains

comfortably extended. There is no apparent wrist hinge, though some golfers find an early setting of the wrists preferable.

3

4

SIDE ON The clubhead follows a rounded shape, moving around the right side. A turning of the shoulders and hips dictates the path, your right knee staying put or moving back a touch. There is no apparent hinging at the wrists. The body turn and arms are very much together as a co-ordinated move, your right elbow just beginning to fold away, tucking slightly downwards and in, definitely not moving away from the body. The weight must move to the right side quite early in response to this turning of the upper body. Feel as though the first move originates from the stomach, thus pushing the right hip around to dictate the correct inside path for the clubhead. Resist this turn with the left side, left leg remaining in place or just beginning to bend, flexing forwards but not moving laterally.

1. An example of a poor position for starting back. Always try to avoid an independent hinging of the wrists early on in the backswing.

2. If you adopt the correct position, as shown in this picture, the upper body and arms will combine to sweep the clubhead back on a fairly low and wide arc. The emhasis is on turning the upper body. Initiate the backswing with the left arm maintaining swing radius. At this point there is no apparent use of the wrists.

3. Correct. The right shoulder turns away to the right side to permit the arms to move the clubhead on an 'inside' path. There is no apparent hinging from the wrists, though the right elbow must begin to soften from here on.

4. Incorrect. The club has been taken back too straight and the vital turning of the shoulders is absent. An effective swing must follow the 'inside' path and move around the body, even at this early stage in the backswing.

HALFWAY BACK

SIDE ON The inside path continues as the body turn dictates that the club should move around the body, while the right knee remains flexed and the left bends a touch, pointing in the direction of the ball. The shoulders are half turned, the right hip is still encouraged to move back with the weight felt mainly over that heel. As the wrists begin to hinge, the shaft finds its slot, parallel to the ball-to-target line. The cluhead should be positioned so that the toe end faces upwards, but more specifically, the face of the club must look slightly downwards too. The leading edge of the clubface should point to 11.30 on an imaginary clock face. If the clubhead is vertical, it indicates that there has been too much rotation of the wrists.

FACE ON The shaft at horizontal is a key backswing position, confirming several points that affect the position at the top, and the downswing. The shoulders have continued to turn away to the right side, around the body, pushing the weight gradually towards the right heel. The hips respond, turning around 20 degrees, and the shoulders turn at least twice this. The wrists now hinge more noticeably, the right not only cocking a touch but folding back on itself, beginning to set this important angle. The left arm is comfortably extended, not straight or rigid. The right continues to fold away, elbow tucking in towards the hip.

1. Halfway back, with the toe end of the clubhead almost vertical and the palm of the right hand facing out. The right arm has folded away to accommodate the elliptical path of the swing.

2. The wrists have rolled the clubface open, the face now looking half skywards. This in turn has positioned the shaft excessively around the body on too flat a backswing plane.

3. Correct. The left arm maintains swing radius by staying comfortably extended whilst the right arm has begun to fold noticeably.

4. Incorrect. The right elbow has left the player's right side.

CONTINUING THE BACKSWING

FACE ON As the club swings up, it passes out of view – this position depends upon what has gone before and it also relies on two key movements. Firstly, the shoulders must continue to turn away, the left working down to hold your upper body posture constant as the right moves around, by now dictating an 80-degree turn. Secondly and simultaneously, the arms must swing the club noticeably upwards, left arm extending as the right

1. The left arm swings the club upwards in the second half of the backswing. The shoulders continue to turn and the legs resist.

2. Incorrect. An over-rotation of the shoulders forces the club around the body too much and the right leg straightens.

3. A good backswing position. The shoulders must really turn at this stage, whilst the left arm has to swing the club more upwards. The left knee works towards the ball and some flexibility must be maintained in the right throughout.

4. This incorrect position has come about because there was not enough shoulder turn in the second half of the backswing, thereby forcing the club into an upright position. This swing is likely to lack power because of the weakness of its pivot.

elbow folds more downwards, holding it in towards your side. To help the swing remain 'together' or co-ordinated, both elbows must remain fairly close to one another.

The right shoulder turn stretches the muscles in the left side. The right knee contains the pivot, remaining flexed throughout. The left knee continues to work towards the ball or just behind it. The weight must be felt on the heel of the right and toes of the left foot. Weight transference is rotational, not so much from side-to-side but moving around in response to the upper body pivot.

SIDE ON The spine angle is maintained as the upper body pivots around it, working the left shoulder under the chin. This is a positive turning of the shoulders, with no intention of tilting or pointing the shoulder at the ball. The turn is a simple one, at right angles to the spine. The elbows work fairly close to one another, the right really tucked in and directed mostly downwards. The arms must now swing the club upwards, effectively steepening the plane as the wrists continue to cock upwards. The shaft starts to find its optimum position over the joint of the right

shoulder, left wrist fairly flat to control the clubface, right wrist folded back on itself and fully set. Again, resist with your lower body, left knee still bending towards the ball, right leg containing the turn and remaining flexed, though not as much as before.

COMPLETING THE BACKSWING

FACE ON The top of the backswing is a key position from which you can reverse the action and return the clubhead to the ball correctly. As the backswing is completed, the wrists remain constant as the shoulders turn more fully, really stretching the muscles across the back and shoulders. A full pivot involves a 90-degree shoulder turn, the hips turning half this amount. The left arm must maintain full radius whilst not being straight or tense. It can actually fold a touch at the elbow and still retain control. The weight transference has resulted in the head moving right and shoulders also turning slightly behind the ball. The head is unlikely to remain still, and should respond to the turning of the shoulders, certainly rotating a little.

3

4

SIDE ON The body has continued to turn, pushing the weight into the right heel, ideally leaving the left heel on the ground. Maintain some flex in the right leg. The shaft is positioned over the right shoulder, the left wrist is flat and the right elbow remains tucked, pointing mostly downwards. The shaft should align parallel to the target line or is 'laid off' left. Avoid crossing the line with the shaft unless the swing is particularly long. There is no 'perfect' length to the backswing, but control is easily retained when just short of horizontal. The backswing length is limited by the extent to which you pivot, how high your arms can swing upwards and the amount of wrist hinge. Most importantly, maintain your spine angle throughout, your left shoulder still lower as it turns underneath and around your chin.

---

1. Correct position at the top of the backswing – shoulders fully turned.

2. Incorrect. The weight is hanging too much to the golfer's left.

3. Incorrect. Over-rotation has aligned the shaft to the right of the target.

4. Correct. The shoulders are fully turned, the right elbow is tucked in and the shaft is positioned over the joint of the right shoulder.

STARTING DOWN

FACE ON The first movement of the downswing is a reaction to the last part of the backswing. This ensures the initial move is unhurried and makes it easier to retain swing rhythm. It is important to create a good downward action, arms dropping the shaft into the ideal plane. The weight transference commences the reversal of the backswing, left knee working towards the target. At this position there is a slight sitting down posture, both knees flexed, fully supporting the upper body, weight evenly distributed. The right elbow stays tucked, holding for a moment its top of the backswing position as the lower body dictates. At this stage you have a passive right side and an active left, the left knee being the key movement.

1. Incorrect. The legs are not supporting the upper body, which will cause the hips to slide through too early, leaving the shoulders and arms behind.

2. Correct. The left arm must start the club down whilst the legs assume a semi-sitting position. Notice the fairly wide gap between the knees.

SIDE ON This is the most vital stage of the swing. The right shoulder at the top is capable of initiating the downswing, throwing the swing plane and direction out. Instead, the right arm is encouraged to tuck more closely to the right side than in the backswing, the back of the right hand retaining the angle set previously. The shaft must flatten a touch as the swing moves to the inside path, with a sensation of it looping behind you, bearing in mind that it will recover before impact as the hips unwind. At this point, the shaft should point towards an extension of the target line, confirming the plane is correct. The most dominant action is from the legs, left knee opening out as it moves towards the target. There should be a slight lagging of the club, the right wrist in particular staying passive while the lower body moves in preparation for the second stage. The left arm falls into position but must not dominate.

3. Incorrect. A 'hit instinct' throws the right shoulder around far too early, the shaft now moving away from the golfer to the 'outside' path. From here it must move across the intended target line, pulling the ball left or slicing it to the right.

4. The correct position for starting down. The right shoulder holds back momentarily whilst the left arm swings the club downwards. The legs must both assume a mild sitting position to best retain the body angles.

HALFWAY DOWN

FACE ON This is a key position to identify and practise. The shaft is parallel to the ground, right wrist still folded back on itself to delay the release until it is most effective. The legs have assumed a slight 'sitting down' position, the left knee continuing to work towards the target and widening the space between the legs. Your weight must be evenly distributed, or just favouring the left side, giving the most stable base for the upper body as it turns. The left arm is extended without being straight or rigid, whilst the right elbow remains close to the right side of the body. From this view, the shoulders are seen to hold back whilst the lower body dominates. The hips face the ball but the shoulders remain partially turned to the right side, thereby ensuring that the head is kept behind the ball.

SIDE ON From this viewpoint, there are several important points to develop and practise which dictate the flight and direction of the ball. The shaft is both horizontal and parallel to the ball-to-target line, the right wrist is still folded back and the right elbow tucked towards the body. Although the left arm has swung downwards and widened the gap between it and the right shoulder, the upper body holds back whilst the lower body moves left and turns. The hips are now facing the ball. The leading edge of the clubface should point to a position comparable to 11.30 on a clock face, but it should not be vertical. The clubhead is in a position to approach the back of the ball from the 'inside path', moving from around the body in the ideal way to fire the ball forwards.

1. Incorrect. The wrists have uncocked early in the downswing. This is extremely likely to affect clubhead speed and will probably result in the ball being hooked to the left of the target.

2. Correct. The right elbow has returned to the player's side whilst the right wrist has maintained its angle. The weight is centred, or just slightly to the left side.

3. Incorrect. The right shoulder has dominated and the shaft of the club has now been forced outside the ideal line.

4. Correct. The ideal position to deliver the clubhead into the back of the ball. Notice the right wrist angle and the tuck of the elbow. From this position the club shaft finds its optimum position parallel to the ball-to-target line.

IMPACT

FACE ON Logically, the point of impact is the most important part of the swing, though reliant on previous positions. Once the downswing is set in motion and certainly once past halfway down, it is almost impossible to steer or manipulate the clubhead into the correct position. Impact is the moment of truth, where the clubface must be under control and the swing direction coincides with the target line. This is not the address

1. At impact the weight must be to the player's target side as the shoulders and hips continue to turn left.

2. Correct. Weight left, eyes over the ball and both arms extended.

position revisited. The weight is mostly on the left side, the left leg gradually straightening as the right knee is pulled across. The right heel has left the ground. The shoulders have unwound but the head remains temporarily back, eyes still focused on the ball. The wrists have fully released, centrifugal force pulling them into line so the arms, hands and shaft return as they were at the address position. There is no intentional release and no hitting with the right hand.

SIDE ON The clubhead has approached from the inside path to meet the back of the ball, the wrists having fully released. The shoulders have become involved between halfway down and impact, turning over the hips and legs as the right side unwinds. This is a powerful action which adds to clubhead speed. The shoulders effectively catch up with the hips, and at impact both align to the left before the shoulders continue to dominate past impact, overtaking the hip turn. The clubface is controlled by the left wrist staying firm and the right retaining just a touch of angle, with the feeling of holding the face at the target momentarily through the impact area. The right elbow stays close to the right side and resists the right shoulder coming over the top and dominating, which would pull the ball left.

3. Incorrect. The left wrist is leading the clubhead, forcing the face open. The shoulders will rotate left too early, badly timing the impact.

4. Incorrect. The weight is positioned too far to the player's right and the back foot has been placed too firmly down when it should be half raised.

HALFWAY THROUGH

1. Correct. The right arm is fully extended past impact whilst the left folds enough to accommodate the arm rotation throughout the hitting area.

2. The incorrect position at halfway through. Both arms have pulled inwards, an error common to novice golfers. The result is usually a topped shot.

FACE ON Key swing positions occur at halfway through the swing. These positions result from previous movements, but getting things right at this stage will ensure the clubhead is applied correctly at impact. Halfway through largely mirror-images halfway down. The right has now become the extended arm as the left elbow has folded slightly downwards and in towards the left hip. The shaft is once again parallel to the ball-to-target line and horizontal. The toe end of the clubhead points upwards as the right hand has rotated over throughout the hitting area. The body turn is together at this stage with both hips and shoulders working together to turn left. The left hip must dominate, moving back towards the heel to transfer weight around. The shoulders continue to turn, pulling the swing arc gradually around the body. The right shoulder remains low throughout, working around and under the chin through impact. The spine angle is retained after the ball has left the clubface.

3. The club shaft must continue past impact to move through its optimum position, parallel to the ball-to-target line. The toe end of the clubhead points skywards, influenced by the slight folding of the player's left arm. The head remains fixed at this point, eyes still watching the point of impact.

4. If the left arm remains too straight, the clubhead will be open as it is forced through. This fault is indicated by the face of the club being directed partially skywards at halfway through.

SIDE ON The clubhead has moved gradually around the body as part of the swing plane. The right arm is pulled into an extended position by centrifugal force, but the left arm must begin to fold away to control the clubface. The left leg is moving weight more to the heel whilst the right knee is pulled across, the right heel further lifting from the ground. There should be a definite feeling of turning the body left, hands staying passive past impact. The upper body must stay in position, the spine angle maintained with the feeling of the right shoulder working around and under the chin. The eyes still focus on the ball at this point, but this should not be confused with an intention to 'keep the head down'.

THREE-QUARTERS THROUGH

SIDE ON The shaft must mirror the start of the downswing, staying in plane. An extension of the shaft coincides with the target line. The right shoulder remains low as the spine angle is retained, with no hint of lifting too soon. Both arms are working towards the target but the left must fold away to accommodate the follow-through. The club continues to move around the body as the shoulders and hips turn that way, determining that the shaft arrives over the joint of the left shoulder beyond this position. The back of the left wrist now begins to fold back on itself, just as the right folded going back. Feel the right arm swinging the clubhead upwards to generate the height in the follow-through. The roundness of the swing is accomplished by the turning of the body.

1. Correct. The right arm is still extended, while the left arm is beginning to fold away to enable the wrists to hinge. At this point the weight begins to shift to the target side.

2. Incorrect. Both arms have collapsed, the weight is on the back foot and the right shoulder has been held back.

FACE ON This swing position is reliant upon previous swing movements. The right arm maintains the radius by staying extended whilst the left arm begins to noticeably fold away. There is extension past impact which makes the swing arc appear very wide, though this is not conscious. Indeed, the left upper arm should maintain a slight contact with the side of the chest, the left arm fold permitting this. The right shoulder is still low to retain the initial posture and prevent the body lifting early, topping or thinning the shot. The hips and shoulders are still turning and both almost face the target. Weight transference is still taking place, the left leg nearing straight as the right knee almost meets the left. The right heel continues to lift with only the toe in contact with the ground.

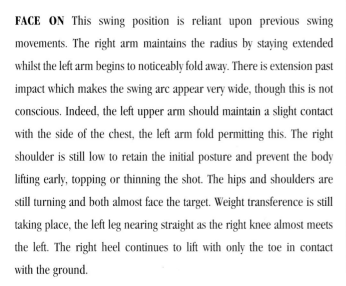

3. Incorrect. The player's right arm has swung artificially upwards. The shoulders need to turn more in order to ensure that they move to the left of the target past impact.

4. The correct position at three-quarters through. The shoulders have turned more, giving a flatter right arm position and enabling the head to rotate more freely.

THE COMPLETED FOLLOW-THROUGH

SIDE ON As confirmation of everything that has gone before, the follow-through is important and errors here have a habit of spreading backwards until they affect impact. The shaft is located over the joint of the left shoulder. Both arms are folded, but the right is still the more extended as the left elbow forms a tight angle. Both elbows must remain fairly close to one another. The hands should finish at head height or just above. The shaft should ideally finish behind the neck, angled partially downwards and almost matching the shaft angle at three-quarters through. The spine angle will have changed, lifting a touch, but the right shoulder must be lower, confirming the upper body position remaining essentially the same. The weight is on the left heel, the right toe in contact with the ground to keep balance.

1. Incorrect. The right shoulder is too high.

2. Correct. A completed follow-through – weight fully on the target side.

FACE ON The shoulders have really turned in the latter part of the forward swing and now face partially behind, though the hips fully face the target. The left leg is straight and the knee locked whilst the right knee has fully moved across to touch the left. Only the toe of the right foot remains in contact with the ground. The right shoulder still remains low, but the upper body will now have lifted out of its original posture. The spine angle should remain constant until this final position has been achieved. Balance is maintained until the ball has landed. Hold this position or recoil by dropping the arms in front of the chest after a moment or two.

3. A good follow-through. The right shoulder remains down and dictates the correct angle for the shaft as it locates behinds the golfer's neck.

4. Incorrect. The arms have collapsed, forcing the shaft too far downwards.

The Hitting Area

CONTROLLING IMPACT

Every golf shot you hit, good or bad, straight or crooked, is influenced by five impact factors or ball flight laws. They are, in no specific order, clubface position, swing direction, angle of approach, 'centredness' of strike and clubhead speed. Impact is brief. Research by Titleist informs us that it lasts around 500 microseconds. In the time it takes you to blink your eye, 700 ball impacts could occur. It is during this time that the ball's flight, trajectory, distance, backspin and sidespin are determined.

Watching and analyzing the ball's flight after impact can give you important information about key errors in the swing. Take a common example. Many golfers hit left to right, the ball curving away in flight. From observing the ball flight, you know the clubface must be in an open position at impact. This logically tells you to check your clubface aim and grip first, then focus on the clubface control throughout your swing. The complication is assessing whether there is an additional aiming fault and/or swing direction compensation which may hide the original clubface error. This would need to be checked by a teaching professional, but an understanding of impact factors may help you diagnose your problem.

Impact is too fast for the human eye, so spotting errors is very difficult. There is no chance to manipulate the clubface into the ideal position. Once your downswing has begun, the brain should be programmed to go, to accelerate the club and swing through to a complete follow-through. Emphasis, therefore, must be placed on the very first movement of the downswing, as this is most influential on the ball strike and its direction. Once set in motion, the clubhead easily stays

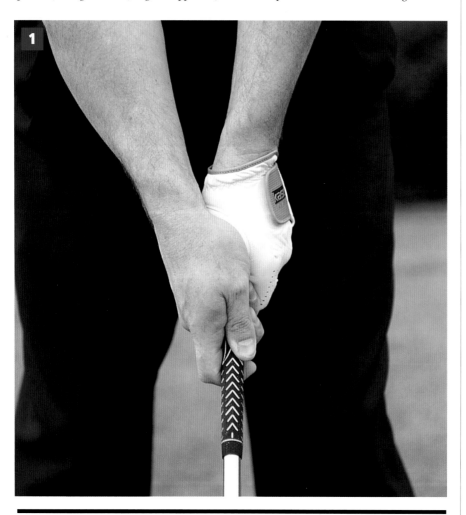

1. The grip is a crucial factor in controlling impact. If the ball is curving away in flight, check your grip, as the position of your hands on the club will influence the clubface position at impact.

2. When using an iron, collect the ball as you swing through the hitting area and remove a shallow divot to ensure you hit the centre of the clubhead.

3. Employ a steeper swing when playing from the rough.

on this path, moving in a constant orbit, collecting the ball as it travels through impact.

However, there are a number of techniques that can assist you in controlling impact. Firstly, use the back of your left hand to control the impact – feel it pulling through and staying constant. Resist any tendency to collapse it just prior to striking the ball as this would hook the shot left.

Secondly, swing from the 'inside' path, so the clubhead approaches the back of the ball from around the body. This produces an on-line swing direction at impact.

Thirdly, hit with your right side just prior to impact, your hand, lower arm, hip and shoulder combining to move through impact as a single unit. This ensures a high degree of power in the shot and is easily repeated.

Fourthly, create a shallow angle of approach. This is essential with woods and longer irons, and is preferable with middle to short irons. The swing should be flat bottomed, approaching the ball on a wide arc and continuing on past impact with an extension of the right arm. Don't approach impact too steeply by delaying the release in your downswing.

Lastly, practise clubface control, identifying the optimum position for the clubface at halfway down and again at its mirror-imaged halfway through point. If correct at each stage, the impact position looks after itself.

CHECKPOINTS

● Control impact by holding your left wrist in a constant position through impact, not permitting it to collapse.

....

● Keep your swing shallow enough to sweep the ball away, removing a shallow divot with iron clubs.

....

● Control the clubface using the reference points at halfway down and halfway through.

CLUBFACE CONTROL

Clubface control is the most important of the ball flight laws. It is most critical when putting, chipping and hitting shots with less lofted clubs, especially the driver.

An open clubface at impact, depending upon its severity, causes the ball to fade or slice. A closed clubface at impact causes the ball to draw or hook. Stop at each swing reference point to check your position and compare it to the ideal. Once the square or neutral positions are recognized, link them together as part of the completed swing.

At your address position, the clubface should be at 90 degrees to the target line. This is difficult to judge from the player's viewpoint, so ask a friend to confirm it until you can recognize it for yourself.

At halfway back, shaft parallel to the ground, a line drawn across the leading edge of the clubface should point at 11.30 on an imaginary clock face. Golfers are frequently told to point the toe end of the clubface vertically at this point, which would be fractionally open. The worst backswing will involve an independent wrist hinge and rotation, rolling the clubface to point partially skywards. Normally, if the clubface is neutral halfway into the backswing it finds the correct position at its completion. The key to a good backswing is to set it off in the correct shape, co-ordinating the arm swing with an upper body turn. Most poor backswings go wrong well before the club reaches its furthest point. A neutral clubface will direct the leading edge to roughly 5 o'clock, and

1. The key to clubface control is to identify the optimum position and make sure it is achieved at halfway back.

2. Incorrect. The left wrist is concave, forcing the clubface into an open position at the top of the backswing.

3. The left wrist and lower arm have formed a straight line, making it possible to control the clubface at this awkward stage when the clubface is out of sight to the player.

this should be more or less in line with your left arm and wrist when viewed from behind.

A neutral clubface halfway into your downswing should be the same as halfway back. The leading edge should again be at 11.30 on the clock face, even though your body position will have altered, the lower body now turned more towards the target and your right elbow more tucked.

CHECKPOINTS

● The open clubface produces side spin, causing the ball to fade or slice. A closed clubface hooks the ball left.

● Check that your clubface is positioned square before you swing back.

● Review your swing to confirm each neutral clubface position, with particular attention at halfway down.

● Watch your ball flight to judge the clubface position at the moment of impact.

The correct release will move a neutral clubface at halfway down into a square clubface for impact, with control and repetition. Your lower arms, wrists and hands must combine with the turning action of the body to return the clubface to its original position, assuming a straight ball flight is required. This is controlled by the back of the left wrist, which should lead the clubface until past impact. Watch the flight. If the clubface is square, the ball flight is straight. If the ball fades or slices, you can tell to what extent the clubface is open. If it hooks or draws, the clubface must be closed.

SWING DIRECTION

Swing direction is the path that the clubhead follows as it moves through the hitting area, beginning at hip height in the downswing through to its corresponding position halfway through. By making a slow, half-length swing you will be able to see the clubhead approach the ball from around the body, coincide with the target line and then continue around the body once more. This 'neutral' swing direction will result in a straight and successful ball flight, assuming that the clubface is square at the point of impact.

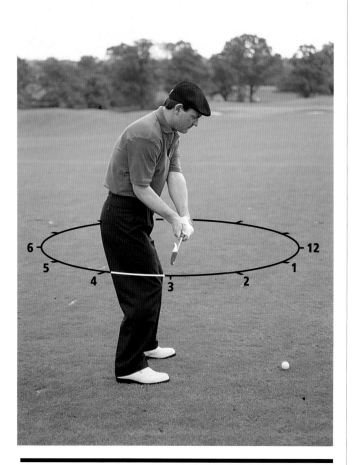

1. At halfway down, the shaft should be parallel to the ball-to-target line or at 3 o'clock on an imaginary clock face.

The swing direction is not part of the arc of a circle, but is more an elliptical shape. Impact should occur whilst the clubhead travels along this elongated section of the arc. It should, therefore, be relatively easy to make a consistent on-line swing.

It is difficult to analyse your swing direction due to the speed of the swing at that crucial stage, but observing the ball flight will assist. Even this poses problems, because the ball flight is more the result of clubface position than swing direction.

Imagine a clock face around your hips, 12 o'clock being straight ahead, 3 o'clock to your right side. The shaft of the club should coincide with 3 o'clock at halfway down, moving to 9 o'clock at halfway through, resulting in an on-line swing. Should you move the shaft across the line from 'outside-to-inside' it will pass through 2 o'clock and continue to the corresponding 8 o'clock position past impact. This shot will fly straight left or slice to the right, depending upon the clubface position. Conversely, moving your shaft through 4 o'clock and 10 o'clock will push the ball right or hook it left, the swing direction travelling from 'inside-to-outside'.

Control over swing direction is best learned or checked by looking at the complete swing. Start by identifying the ideal swing direction. At halfway into your downswing, the club shaft should be both parallel to

CHECKPOINTS

● The swing direction should coincide with the target line at impact.

● Position the ball left of centre in your stance for every club.

● The swing direction is most influenced by the shaft at halfway down which should be parallel to the target line.

● Mirror-image this at halfway through to check the swing has remained on-line.

2. Incorrect. The right shoulder has unwound prematurely and as a consequence the shaft is now 'outside' the intended line.

3. The shaft has crossed over at the top of the target line and is aligned to the right of the target line.

the ground and the target line, your right elbow tucked in towards the body, weight evenly distributed. Simply let the club swing down and through, moving the shaft into a mirror-imaged position on the other side. If the ball is correctly positioned in your stance, this swing direction will coincide with the target line at impact. The key to an on-line swing direction is to position the shaft correctly halfway into your downswing.

The downswing plane will influence the swing direction. This is determined by the angle of the shaft at your address position, the distance you stand from the ball and your upper body posture. As you

swing, the shaft angle can be checked at key reference points, most notably halfway back, the top of the backswing, halfway down, impact and corresponding positions going through. Start your downswing by co-ordinating your arm swing, hip rotation and weight transference, which should initially pull the butt end of the club downwards. The shaft will be directed at the ground, pointing at an extension of the target line behind the ball early in your downswing, confirming good plane. This early move is most likely to drop the shaft into the neutral position at halfway down.

ANGLE OF APPROACH

1

The clubhead must approach impact from an optimum angle to transmit the maximum clubhead speed to the ball. The angle of approach must generally be shallow so that the clubhead can strike the very back of the ball. It should also be steep enough to ensure the ball is struck first, not the grass on which it sits; particularly relevant when playing iron shots from the fairway. It influences the distance a ball will travel. A steep swing chops downward more at impact, reducing distance by failing to find the back of the ball with a shallow clubhead approach into impact. To maximize clubhead speed when driving, your swing should produce an ascending strike at impact if you pre-set your weight favouring your right side. Position the ball left of centre in your stance, but still inside your left heel.

CHECKPOINTS

● Try to create an ascending strike when driving by positioning more weight to your right side at your set-up.

....

● Use a constant ball position to develop consistency in the angle of approach.

....

● Create downswing width by encouraging your right arm to straighten gradually throughout the downswing.

1. To maximize clubhead speed the clubhead must approach impact on a wide swing arc.

2. Skilled golfers often play the driver further forwards and sweep the ball off the tee.

3. Use a steep angle of approach from the rough to prevent grass being trapped between the clubface and the ball.

This combination of ball position and weight distribution will direct your clubhead most solidly into the back of the ball.

There are other ways to influence the angle of approach. Your swing must be wide enough in its arc. This is most effectively achieved by swinging on the correct swing path, the clubhead moving from around your right side to travel down the target line at impact before continuing around your body in the forward swing. This on-line swing requires your shoulders and hips to remain mostly facing the ball for impact. If the swing were outside-to-inside in shape, your shoulders would be open and therefore more to your left

side and ahead of ideal. This swing would be much steeper, dictated by the body being more ahead of the club at impact. The opposite applies when swinging from inside-to-outside, normally associated with pushed or hooked shots. Your shoulders would be to the right of target at impact to accommodate the swing direction, the base of the swing arc falling behind the ball. If the ground were not struck before the ball, the shot would be topped or thinned as the clubhead ascended beyond its lowest point.

The golf ball position is also important. The ball should be positioned at the base of the swing arc, and since repetition is a key

objective in developing your swing there is just one base, usually located left of centre, about 4 inches (10 cm) inside your left heel. Establish this at your address position by starting with your feet together and then step this distance off your left heel. Adjust your right foot for the club being used, forming a narrow stance for lofted clubs and a wider stance for longer irons and woods. The optimum strike, hitting slightly down with irons and driving with an ascending strike, is controlled by minor weight adjustments at your set-up. This ensures an angle of approach which is practical across the range of clubs and a simple, repetitive set-up.

CENTRE CONTACT AND CLUBHEAD SPEED

1

Every golfer realizes the importance of striking the ball from the 'sweet spot' of the clubface. The effect of a centre contact with both woods and irons is identical, the impact feeling very solid and the ball flying furthest. Off-centre contacts give mixed results: in the case of iron shots, the ball tends to stay more or less on target, though losing significant distance, whereas shots played with wooden clubs lose distance and deviate from straight. This difference arises from the design of clubheads. An iron clubhead is thin, like a blade. The centre of mass of the clubhead must take into account the metal in the hosel, so a ball struck from fractionally towards the neck of centre will be struck most solidly. The further towards the toe end you contact the shot, the more distance you will lose. The same partially applies to shots that are struck towards the hosel of the club, where there is a point at which a shank occurs.

Wooden clubs have a different shape to the iron clubhead, as they are more rounded at the back and with the centre of mass located further behind the ball. The centre of mass with an iron club is virtually in line with the hitting face. A centre contact with a wooden club will position the mass directly behind the ball, sending the ball straight. A toe-end contact will cause the heel to continue, opening the face and applying anticlockwise spin which causes hooks.

CHECKPOINTS

● Clubhead speed should be controllable, maximized for full shots but infinitely variable for touch shots on and around greens.

● Your swing must be long enough and have sufficient width to its arc.

● A well co-ordinated swing is more important than pure physical strength.

1. Distance is maximized when the clubhead accelerates through the downswing, and the ball is struck from the centre of the clubface.

The distance the ball travels is largely dependent upon clubhead speed at impact. Don't limit your understanding to full shots, where your intention is to maximize this, but also consider the shorter shots where clubhead speed must be carefully controlled, because obviously it still affects the distance a ball travels, whether in the flight, bounce and roll from a lofted shot or just the rolling of a putt. The clubhead must always accelerate through the downswing into impact, whether the swing is full or the shot requires a shorter backswing.

In the full swing, clubhead speed is a compromise between control and power. When using the driver, it is not enough to power the ball away with no control over the quality of strike, direction and repetition.

There are a number of ways to maximize clubhead speed for impact. Firstly, you should use a full backswing. Secondly, your swing must have enough width, maximized by extending your left arm going back and your right past impact. Thirdly, you must use your muscles efficiently, setting a wrist angle going back, lagging the club into the hitting area and rotating your right hand over to release. Fourthly, your physical strength and height will hugely influence clubhead speed, but only if applied in conjunction with an orthodox, controllable swing. Lastly, the clubhead must be applied most solidly into the back of the ball, swinging along the target line with a square clubface.

2. Delay the release action by holding your wrist angle constantly at the early stages of the downswing.

3. 'Swish' the grip end of the club, holding it with the right hand to promote the feeling of acceleration.

2

3

Shotmaking Skills

DRIVING

Good driving sets you up for lower scores. Every hole has an optimum strategy dictated by the distance to the green, the placement of fairway bunkers, the width of the fairway, the severity of the rough on either side and the presence of contours which could make execution of the second shot difficult. There is an ideal route to the pin, not necessarily from the centre of the fairway, so position your tee shot accordingly.

1

1. A 'square' body alignment and good posture are critical when using longer, less lofted clubs.

You would normally select the 1-wood, having some 10, 11 or 12 degrees of loft and the longest shaft, to fire the ball forwards for maximum distance. Many golfers prefer the 3-wood or even 1-iron as standard, sacrificing distance for accuracy.

Pick the spot that you are aiming for, visualize the shot and set up to the ball. Give yourself a couple of practice swings and try to feel the rhythm of the swing.

The ball should be located opposite your left heel or just right of this, your weight just favouring your right side to encourage a slightly ascending strike for impact. Programme your swing by moving the club back a couple of times. A hinging of the wrists is best, emulating the action of your right wrist folding back on itself as it will near the top of your backswing. This mimics the sensation of a backswing without losing the feeling of being still at your set-up.

Set your swing in motion. Turn your shoulders full to your right side as the key movement. Brace your right leg to resist this turning of the

CHECKPOINTS

● Think about the ideal position to place your drive on the fairway.

....

● Use your driver to achieve maximum distance, but consider a more lofted wood or even a 1-iron for added control.

....

● Widen your stance and set more weight on your right side to encourage an ascending strike.

....

● Turn fully and make a complete swing, with no attempt to hit at the ball.

2. Turn fully to achieve the horizontal position with the shaft at the top.

3. In the follow-through you must also turn fully, with your right knee pulling across as the left leg straightens.

upper body, maintaining the right knee flex as much as possible. Feel your weight shift to your right side, felt mostly at your right heel as the top of the backswing nears. Allow your wrists to hinge as your backswing progresses, your left wrist controlling the clubface by being flat, the right folding back on itself.

Make a smooth transition into your downswing, avoiding the tendency to apply a 'hit' using the bigger muscles in your shoulders. Feel your left arm dominate as your right elbow drops close to your right side. From halfway down, the right side releases, weight transferring as the shoulders unwind. Complete the follow-through, as if it were a practice swing that the ball happened to 'get in the way of'. Hold your follow-through to promote balance and control. Hold this position until the ball has landed.

The swing for driving is, of course, no different from that used for other clubs in the set. The flattish plane is dictated by the lower angle of the shaft at the address position. You simply turn fully and your arms respond to the pre-determined angles of the shaft and posture. If your swing tends to be up and down, lacking the roundness so vital for the bigger swings, you will approach impact too steeply, resulting in topping, thinning, skying and general inconsistency. It is the positive turning of the shoulders both going back and past impact, maintaining the identical plane each side, which makes for the required shot.

FAIRWAY WOODS

With the ball nestling in fairway grass, with the need to use a long club shaft, and with distance the key objective, you face one of the toughest shots in golf. However, with a sound swing it poses little problem.

A 3-wood is preferable, having some 15 or 16 degrees of loft to give elevation and a clubface deep enough to fire the ball forwards with a low flight, maximizing the bounce and roll. Most club golfers require a 5-wood for the tighter lies, the shallower face making it easier to find the back of the ball and the increased loft giving it a higher trajectory. The 7-wood can also be a valuable alternative to longer irons.

Approach the shot from behind the target line. Picture the flight of the ball, then move around to the address position and take a couple of practice swings. Swing smoothly and quite slowly, letting the weight of the clubhead dictate the pace. As the clubhead passes the impact point, allow the sole to thump the ground. This won't remove turf, but instead just graze the grass. Many golfers fail to do this, often taking a practice swing at too high a level, missing the ground enough to top the ball.

Settle the clubhead down behind the ball, move your feet into position and finalize your grip. The ball should be left of centre in your stance, but not opposite your left foot. Keep your stance fairly wide, about shoulders' width, both toes angled out slightly, weight evenly distributed. Make a couple of pre-swing movements, setting a slight angle in the right wrist whilst moving the club back about 3 feet (1 m), returning the clubhead to the address position each time. This keeps the muscles free of tension and encourages a fluid first movement back.

1. A full and complete backswing turn...

2. ...with the arms dictating the downswing plane.

The swing relies on fully turning your shoulders going back, whilst limiting this upper body pivot by resisting with your right knee, keeping your left heel down. The emphasis must be on turning, your right shoulder starting back by moving away around you, dictating the wrists' position, and the shaft moving over the joint of your right shoulder at the top. Mirror this in the forward swing, keeping your right shoulder low, shaft over your left shoulder, confirming that the club has moved in the same plane throughout.

Many golfers struggle with fairway woods because they fail to turn fully going back, creating an up and down action that drops the clubhead steeply into the ground at the ball. Alternatively, the steeper approach of the clubhead may top or thin the ball. These shots usually lack distance and are sliced right, often compensated for at the address position by aiming left.

The opposite error will also cause problems finding the back of the ball with a clean contact. A swing direction approaching too much from the inside is likely to catch a shallow divot just before impact, smothering the shot. From a tee, this swing would suffice, but with the ball sitting on the grass there is too little room for error.

CHECKPOINTS

● Take practice swings to establish the correct impact: the sole of the club grazing the grass.

● Use your normal swing, ball positioned left of centre, weight evenly spread at your set-up.

● Turn fully both going back and through, positioning the shaft over the right shoulder at the top, mirroring this the other side.

● Avoid the most common error with these shots – the backswing being too steep and lacking shoulder turn.

3. The clubhead lags as the body positions itself...

4. ...to turn through to face the target.

MAXIMIZING DISTANCE

There is no magical formula that adds distance to your shots, only a collection of positive swing moves.

Keep your address position active. Maintain a light grip, relaxed yet ready to move. Don't let the club sit motionless behind the ball, but instead fold your right wrist back on itself a couple of times to maintain activity. Don't freeze over the ball.

1. Turn your shoulders through 90 degrees going back. Your back should be in a position facing the target, with your left shoulder keeping low and the club shaft over the joint of your right shoulder.

Now focus on your upper body pivot. Position a club shaft across the back of your shoulders, held in place with each hand. Adopt your normal posture, your spine angled forwards and your knees flexed a touch. Now turn as in your backswing. The shaft should have moved through 90 degrees, your hips to 45 degrees, your left knee pointing at or just behind the ball and right knee remaining slightly flexed. Feel your back and shoulder muscles tightening gradually, like the coiling of a spring. Now reverse this action and turn the body through to the follow-through position, shoulders moving through 110 degrees or more, depending on individual flexibility. Shift your hips until they fully face the target past impact, right knee meeting left, right heel fully released from the ground. The full turning of the upper body with partial resistance by the hips and legs is one of the keys to maximizing distance. Coil efficiently going back and, as the body unwinds in sequence, so clubhead speed is produced.

Add to this an efficient weight transference. It is advantageous to position your upper body behind the ball at the top of the backswing, permitting a gradual unwinding of the bigger muscles as the clubhead approaches impact, weight moving in the same direction. At the top,

CHECKPOINTS

● Keep your address position light and active, without excessive body tension.

● Pivot fully going back, turning your shoulders through 90 degrees

● Resist the backswing turn by limiting your hip turn and leg action.

● Swing down and through with a free arm swing and complete your follow-through.

● Learn to hit from the inside path, ideally drawing the ball to maximize distance.

your lower spine should have remained in position: your upper body now inclined to the right side, with your weight not just on the right side, but felt predominantly in the heel. As the club slots into the halfway down position, the weight centralizes as your lower body assumes a semi-squatting position, both knees flexed. Now the right side takes over, your right shoulder gradually riding over and forcing the upper body to move target side until the weight is fully over the left side, leg braced, hip pushed back until the weight is felt over the left heel.

To make the most of the clubhead speed you have generated, swing from the inside path, with the clubhead approaching impact from around your right side, seemingly swinging away to your right side with an inside-to-outside path through impact. This swing direction promotes a more shallow angle of approach, the sole of the clubhead being nearer to the ground than usual, which is advantageous as it fully strikes the middle of the ball or lower part of the ball. If the clubface is fractionally closed to this swing direction, though it might well be square to the target line, the ball will draw, shaping a touch from right to left in flight. Closing the clubface reduces the effective loft, firing the ball lower and therefore further, shaping the ball for maximum distance with more bounce and roll on landing.

2. To get maximum distance from your shots you must develop a sound upper body pivot. Practise your pivot by placing the shaft of a golf club across your shoulders, holding it in place with both hands. Adopt your swing position and turn as in your backswing. The shaft position at the top of the backswing indicates the extent of your turn – ideally it should have moved through 90 degrees.

3. To maximize the clubhead speed generated by your upper body pivot, you must make sure that the clubface approaches impact on the correct path. Swing wide from an inside path, approaching impact from your right side to preserve a shallow, flat-bottomed swing arc as shown. The resulting angle of approach will maximize distance as the clubhead strikes the middle of the ball.

THE POWER FADE

1. Aim left, align your body to the left and swing in accordance with your set-up. The ball will start to the left of the target, and the tree, and will fade back.

This shot moves 'slightly' from left to right in the air. The ball will tend to fly a little higher than normal but land softly and stay on the fairway rather than shoot forward, possibly running into trouble.

There are three reasons why a fade is advantageous over a straight shot. Firstly, some players are prone to hooking, and learning to fade the ball will prevent this most damaging shot occurring. Secondly, many find the fade more controllable on narrow courses. It offers more predictability over the draw and even straight shots. Thirdly, a fade will move the ball around intervening trees and other obstacles, either to shape a shot around a gentle dog-leg right hole or to offer a better recovery if the path to your approach is blocked .

You will need to make two adjustments to your normal golf swing to fade the ball. You must align your whole body, your shoulders, hips, knees and feet some 10 degrees to the left so that your golf swing shape is dictated by this adjustment. The golf ball will now start its flight to the left of the target. You pre-set the open clubface before setting the swing in motion. Open the clubface at the address position: leaving it square to the target whilst aligning the body to the left. Move your right hand a touch further to your left – more on top of the club. Swing normally until the club shaft is parallel to the ground, halfway into your downswing. At this point, the clubface will point upwards. As you move the club through impact, feel your hips and legs rotate towards the target whilst the back of your left hand maintains the clubface control,

CHECKPOINTS

● Align your body to the left.

● Set your clubface square to the target at your set-up, or open to the intended swing direction.

● Move your right hand further over at your set-up.

● Hold back with your release, using your right hand to preserve the clubface position.

keeping it slightly open and preventing your right hand crossing over too early. Halfway into your forward swing, check that the toe end of the club is vertical, the face looking a touch upwards, compared with a square position where the face would be directed slightly downwards. This mildly open clubface at impact will impart the necessary side spin on the ball to make it curve back to the flagstick in the air.

Practise this shot before you attempt to play it on the golf course. It takes a while to accustom yourself to the strange sensation of aligning the body to the left of the target, and holding the hands and wrists through impact to produce the open clubface that is needed to gain the necessary control. The control is principally in your right hand, so focus on its role, holding back with the release until well beyond impact. Both arms should extend in the forward swing to prevent your left arm folding downwards, as this would roll the face square or closed.

A fade tends to fly higher than a straighter shot, so select one or two clubs less lofted to compensate. Lofted clubs produce so much backspin that any side spin from the open clubface is oveerrided. This shot is reserved for middle to longer irons and woods.

2. Hold your clubface open throughout impact and beyond, working the face more skywards at halfway through.

3. Keep the back of your left hand moving at the target, thus opening the clubface at impact to apply the all-important sidespin to the ball.

THE CONTROLLED DRAW

The controlled draw moves the ball from right to left. It has two applications. Firstly, it's ideal when trees prevent a straight shot at the flagstick. Secondly, the shape of the shot is suitable for novices through to established golfers, offering extra distance and good solid shots. The better player often finds it difficult to hit the controlled draw consistently and would do better to limit the shot to bending the ball around intervening trees. The faster, more powerful hands and wrists of the low handicapper may turn the clubface causing it to become closed at impact, hooking the ball out of control.

The ball will tend to fly lower than normal and run further on landing, so if you are playing to a specific distance you may need to select a more lofted club to compensate. Start by aiming the clubface squarely to the ball-to-target line and aligning your body around 10 degrees to the right of the target. Move your left hand more to the right, or more 'strongly-on the club'. If your normal grip shows two and a half knuckles from the front view, look

CHECKPOINTS

● Only your address position needs to be altered – swing normally thereafter.

● Set your clubface squarely to the target, your body aligned to the right.

● Move your left hand to your right, into a 'stronger' position.

● Encourage your swing to approach from the inside path, rotating your right hand over your left to turn the clubface closed for impact.

1. Aim where you wish the ball flight to start, align your body parallel to this and turn both hands more to your right than normal. The ball will curve to the left in the air and run further than usual upon landing.

2. The curve on the ball is applied by the clubface returning in a closed position at impact. Start off with your hands turned to the right of neutral at your set-up and simply allow them to revert to their natural position for impact.

3. The clubface will turn to look at the ground at halfway through. Encourage lower arm and wrist rotation through the hitting area.

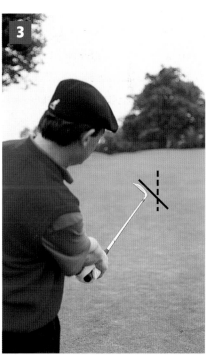

for three or even part of the fourth. This grip adjustment will control your clubface throughout the swing. The palm of your right hand should remain facing the target, though folded around the club, but could also move right to assist clubface control.

Once you have made these alterations at your address position, the swing requires no further conscious alteration. Adjust at your set-up and swing normally. However, your swing will have to accommodate these adjustments, so identifying key points will

ensure you hit a consistent, controlled draw. Encourage the club to move around yourself going back more in response to your closed shoulder alignment, the clubface looking more to the ground at halfway back. The first movement down is critical; your arms must drop to the inside path, working the shaft from a touch behind you. As your downswing approaches impact, the clubhead must move on an exaggerated inside path, from where it must move from inside-to-outside and continue a touch right of target past the ball.

The feeling at impact is that your right hand has rotated over the left. This is most noticeable halfway into the forward swing, where the clubface should be facing partially downwards. Encourage the left arm to fold away more towards the body at this position, and your body will feel as though it holds back a little, while the hips remain facing the ball longer, rather than turning to face the target. At impact, the clubface is slightly closed, so that an anticlockwise spin is imparted to the ball and it curves gently to the left in the air.

Course Skills

FROM THE ROUGH

When deciding how to play from the rough, much depends on the lie. It may be relatively easy to play from, alternatively your best option might be to hack the ball back to the fairway. There is no substitute for careful shot assessment and a realistic approach to tactical play.

1. Position the ball further back in the stance when playing from the rough.

The standard shot is hit higher than normal, gaining height quickly. Aim the clubface directly at the target, but align your shoulders, hips and feet some 10–15 degrees open. The swing direction will be dictated by the shoulder line, moving the clubhead slightly outside-to-inside, with the initial flight of the ball starting left. The sidespin produced by the open clubface will cause the ball to fade towards the target. The swing will be significantly steeper as it approaches the back of the ball, so missing the grass just behind it and producing a cleaner strike. The longer grass tends to close the clubface at impact as it wraps around the hosel, smothering the shot. Starting with the clubface open reduces, or even eliminates, this effect.

Your ball may be lying on a patch where the blades of grass are growing in the direction of play. The danger is that the ball may come out with little backspin, 'fly' the green and land in trouble. Select one, maybe two clubs more lofted, and swing normally, anticipating the lack of bite the ball will have. Conversely, playing against the grain produces much more resistance to the clubhead at impact, reducing clubhead speed significantly. Firm up your grip pressure slightly and anticipate little follow-through as the grass 'grabs' the clubhead.

The second approach to shots from the rough is to punch the ball forwards. Position the ball in the centre, or right of centre of your stance with your hands ahead. You may find it beneficial to move the left hand a little to your right to compensate for the ball position change. The clubface should remain square at the address. Move the weight on to the left side and swing steeply down into the back of the ball. You will have to hinge your

CHECKPOINTS

● Careful shot assessment is critical.

● Don't be over-ambitious and make sure you recover in just one stroke.

● Use a slightly open clubface to add loft, fading the ball left to right.

● Play the ball back in your stance, weight left and hit down more.

● Some situations dictate that the ball must be punched forwards to gain distance.

wrists early in the backswing to encourage this steep angle of attack. The ball will fly out low and fast, chasing up the fairway.

One of the most difficult shots around the green is when the ball sits in long grass, making flight and roll unpredictable. This shot is very similar to a greenside bunker shot, the idea being to cut the long grass away underneath the ball with a lofted club, ideally a sand iron. Set the clubface in a slightly open position and place most of the weight on the left side. Your body must be aligned to the left to compensate for the open clubface hitting the ball to the right of the flag. Break your wrists early in the backswing, keeping it fairly lengthy, though at a slow tempo. Gently accelerate the clubhead through impact and try to follow through as much as possible without turning the clubface over through impact. The ball will fly fairly high and settle quickly, but don't expect any noticeable backspin with this shot.

2. When pitching from the rough, you should hinge your wrists early in the backswing. This encourages the clubhead to approach the ball from a steeper angle.

3. Semi-rough often permits the use of woods, assuming the grass behind the ball will not catch the clubhead as it nears impact.

4. Hold the club a little tighter with your left hand, restrict your backswing and feel your weight hanging more on your left side at the top to encourage a steeper downswing.

U P S L O P E S

1. The correct execution of a greenside pitch. Arm swing is minimal but there is a positive hinging at the wrists.

2. Keep the forward swing short, making sure the left wrist is leading.

A gentle upslope shot will increase the loft of the face at impact, so select one club less to compensate. Little adjustment is necessary in the swing. Position the ball normally in the stance and adjust your body to the slope. Your right shoulder will feel low, your left a touch higher. Your body weight will move to your right side, but not enough to require a compensatory change in stance or swing. Restrict your backswing and so maximize your chances of a solid contact with the ball.

Lofted irons, particularly the pitching wedge and sand iron, require a different approach. These can put the ball so high that distance control becomes a problem. Select a less lofted club, such as an 8-or 9-iron, reducing your swing length accordingly. Again, incline your whole body to the right to encourage a swing that matches the slope, and then play the shot normally.

Try a second option if the wind is against or from the side. Adopt your normal address position but place the weight on your left leg, effectively leaning into the slope. Your spine angle will be vertical, not perpendicular to the slope. Accommodate this by bending your left knee more and angle the toe out. Swing as normal, but don't move the weight to your right side going back, as transferring back is difficult. Feel your weight hang on your left side throughout; this steepens the clubhead's approach at impact. More turf will be taken, the shot driven forward on a normal trajectory.

3. Position your body so that it is perpendicular to the upslope. Your right shoulder should feel noticeably lower than your left.

4. It is important to maintain your stability, so select one or two clubs less lofted and restrict your backswing turn to limit the weight shift.

Steeper upslopes can pose more of a problem. The shot is certain to have plenty of height, so don't reach for your wedge or sand iron. However, maintaining your balance with a full 3-wood would be unrealistic. If there is far to go to the green consider a shot that will leave you with the easiest of approaches for the next stroke.

If you lean into the slope, its severity will cause the clubhead to slam into the ground. A steeper upslope requires your swing to follow the slope as much as possible. The closer to a shallow, sweeping impact area you create, the more likely you are to succeed. Given the lack of stability, your address position must pre-set your body as perpendicular to the slope as possible. Widen your right foot out to assist

and move slightly down the slope, the ball position now opposite your left heel. You may have to aim a touch right to compensate for the ball moving left in flight. Your weight will fall to your right side, the right shoulder feeling very low, the left equally high. Your swing must retain enough stability to control the club until impact, after which you will probably lose balance down the slope because of the impossibility of transferring weight to your left side. A full swing is unrealistic. Select one or two less lofted clubs to compensate, and limit your backswing length to three-quarters, punching the ball forwards. This prevents the shoulders turning fully and pulling you off-balance down the slope at the top of your backswing.

CHECKPOINTS

● From a gentle upslope, select one club less lofted, stand perpendicular to the slope and swing normally.

● For shorter shots, select a less lofted club, and limit your swing length.

● From more severe slopes, stand as perpendicular to the slope as possible. Restrict your backswing length and sweep the ball away, matching your swing arc to the slope as much as possible.

DOWNSLOPES

Even a gentle downslope can cause huge difficulties for the club golfer. The most common error is to strike the ground before the ball – this occurs as the ground comes between clubhead and ball if you use the same swing as for level ground.

First, a gentle fairway downslope, ball sitting up. This demands minor but critical adjustments to enable the swing to follow the slope throughout the impact area. Select one, perhaps two clubs more lofted to compensate for the lower trajectory of the ball flight. Your address position must encourage a steeper approach of the clubhead into impact, so ensuring a solid contact with the ball, ideally taking a shallow divot in the normal way. Move the ball centrally in your stance and stand perpendicular to the slope. Position your upper body further down the slope until your spine angle is at 90 degrees to it. Your right shoulder will feel higher, your left lower. The weight must be to your left side prior to the swing being set in motion. From here, set the wrist angle early in your backswing and try to turn fully. Feel as though the club continues down the slope past impact, ensuring that the weight is fully on the left side. There is a tendency for this shot to drift from left to right in the air, which is most apparent when using the longer irons and woods. Aim left to compensate.

From a gentle downslope, assuming a clean lie, even a 3-wood is possible. However, start with the very lofted irons to build confidence.

STEEP SLOPES The more severe 'hanging lie' downslope is the most difficult of all shots from undulating fairways. This introduces the problem of maintaining balance throughout the shot.

The ball flight will be much lower. If the green is within reach, the problem is not getting there but stopping the ball once it is on the putting surface. Select two, three or even four clubs more lofted than normal for the distance. Avoid the woods and longer irons. These require a shallow swing which is impossible to achieve from such a slope. Limit your selection to the 5-iron through to the wedge.

1. One of the hardest shots on the course. Stand as perpendicular to the slope as possible without losing balance, and position the ball further back in your stance.

CHECKPOINTS

● Select a more lofted club to compensate for the lower ball flight, especially from steeper slopes.

● On a gentle slope, move the ball back in your stance and incline your body perpendicular to the slope.

● From steeper slopes, move the ball further back, adjust your left hand grip and angle your left toe out.

● Limit your backswing length, following the slope as much as possible past impact.

Move the ball back in the stance, opposite the right heel. Compensate for the severely pushed shot by turning your left hand to the right, revealing three and a half or four knuckles. Keep your right palm facing the target, as you would normally. If you fail to adjust your grip, the shot will take off right and drift even more that way. Your upper body must be inclined to your left, enough to steepen the club's approach into impact but not so much as to cause a loss of balance mid-swing. Turn your left foot out and widen your stance further down the slope; bend your right knee more as the weight is set almost fully on the target-side.

Use a three-quarter length backswing initiated by an early hinging of the wrists and steep picking up of the club. Concentrate on the clubhead continuing past impact following the slope for as long as possible. A loss of balance at the end of the swing is likely and you are almost certain to step down the slope to regain balance.

2. Turn fully and encourage an early setting of the wrists in the backswing. Hold your weight on your left side to ensure the ball is struck cleanly – even taking a shallow divot on gentle downslopes.

3. Pitching from a severe downslope. Position the ball opposite your right foot, left foot angled down the slope to aid balance. Hinge your wrists early going back.

STANDING BELOW THE BALL

Of the two sideslopes, the ball above the feet is the easier to play. It demands a shallow swing that approaches impact from around the body. This finds the back of the ball easily, especially when playing with the longer clubs. Anticipate a ball flight that takes off left and drifts further that way. The steeper the sideslope and more lofted the club, the greater this effect. The ball flies left because of an alteration in its lie angle. As the shaft angle flattens to compensate for the slope, the loft angle becomes a directional factor, not just lofting the shot but also dictating the ball's movement to the left. A sand iron played from a severe sideslope, ball above feet, will be most affected – the ball flying considerably left of the original aim. A 3-wood from a gentle sideslope will hardly move left at all.

Experience, or practice, is the key to assessing the amount of compensation you will need to make at the address position for this movement to the left. Good players instinctively know how much allowance to make in aim and body alignment. Set aside time to familiarize yourself with the feeling of such a rounded swing.

From a gentle slope, your club choice should not be affected. Aim to the right and look ahead to the landing position of the ball. This is also likely to be part of the slope, further affecting your compensation. Hold the handle lower down to shorten the swing arc and reduce the amount your body must be repositioned to accommodate the slope. The weight will move towards your heels, dictating that you stand further away to regain necessary stability. From here, swing normally, but be aware of

1. The correct position for pitching from a sideslope with the ball above the feet. Aim a little to the right and feel the backswing follow a flatter line.

2

3

2. Hold the club lower down the grip to shorten the swing width, bending slightly at the knees and standing further away from the ball.

3. Employ a baseball type action for the backswing. Make a flatter turn positioning the left shoulder higher than normal.

CHECKPOINTS

● Anticipate the ball flying left, more so with shorter, more lofted clubs. Allow for this by aiming to the right of target.

....

● Hold the club lower down, and stand more upright and further away to accommodate the slope.

....

● Swing around yourself more, limiting your swing length to maximize control, and strike the ball most solidly.

the whole swing, back and through, moving more around the body and sweeping the ball away.

If the ball finishes on a more severe slope causing you to stand below its level, balance is diminished and the shot becomes more difficult. Hold the club much lower down to shorten the swing width and stand more upright, bending only slightly forwards at your waist. Your weight will move towards your heels, which you should resist by standing further away from the ball and bending your knees forward to compensate. From here, a very flat, rounded swing will naturally follow, the plane governed by the angle of the upper body. A

full swing requires a great deal of skill and plenty of practice to ensure a solid strike, so most golfers would do best to select a club or even two less lofted and limit the backswing to just three-quarter length. Try to punch the shot forwards, holding the clubface square throughout impact by working the back of the left wrist towards the target. Try to keep your head at the same level throughout, resisting the natural tendency to drop the left shoulder to its usual position as the backswing progresses. If you are prone to the hook, this shot can cause huge problems should the right hand roll over the left before impact.

STANDING ABOVE THE BALL

This is the more difficult of the two sideslopes. For the average golfer or novice, it is particularly difficult. Consider the initial problems almost every beginner has with topping shots from a level stance, until the arms have learned to swing downwards. With the ball now lower than a level stance, the problems of finding the back of the ball again arise. Adjust your swing technique and practise this shot to familiarize yourself with the variation in technique.

Anticipate a drifting of the ball from left to right from a gentle slope, and a more noticeable curve as the severity of slope increases. Remember, too, the contours of the ground when the ball bounces and rolls.

From a gentle slope, ball below feet, your club choice should not be affected, the ball travelling its full distance. Adopt your normal address position, but stand slightly closer to the ball, bending at the knees a touch more than normal. Your upper body must bend more forward if the base of your swing arc is to find the very back of the golf ball. Swing normally thereafter, perhaps limiting your backswing length a small amount, which will require one club less lofted. Good golfers should find this shot no trouble if aimed left and allowed to move back onto target, with only minor swing alterations necessary.

1. Stand closer to the ball and hold the club at the very end of the grip.

2. Employ a steeper backswing.

Far more difficult is the severe sideslope standing above the ball. Firstly, the clubhead sits awkwardly, its toe end clearly off the ground making it appear unstable. Secondly, your body weight is pulled down the slope and onto your toes. You must compensate by standing closer and bending backwards through your knees whilst also angling your upper body more over the ball. The set-up will feel cramped with barely enough clearance between your hands and right thigh

CHECKPOINTS

● Anticipate the ball curving to the right and the likelihood of it bouncing and running more that way on landing.

● From gentle sideslopes, hold a touch higher, stand closer and swing normally.

● Steeper slopes require you to stand very close, bending more through your knees to move weight back.

● Limit your swing length and employ a mostly up and down action.

● Pitches from sideslopes require the same adjustments, but lengthen your swing to compensate for the steeper swing.

3

4

to swing the club back. This posture forces a much steeper swing plane, the club moving noticeably more up and down on what feels like a straighter path. You have to concentrate on maintaining your upper body position by holding your head very steady throughout. Resist the tendency to fall forwards in the downswing by striking the ball and then work your weight onto your left heel by the end of your follow-through.

A full swing from such a sideslope is probably too ambitious. The steeper swing will limit clubhead speed too, requiring one or even two clubs less lofted and a swing which is just three-quarter length, punching the ball forwards and retaining control. This is the slicer's nightmare, his already steep swing and open clubface being made worse by the effects of the slope.

3. Aim to the left when pitching from a sideslope like this one. Angle your upper body over the ball. From this position your hands will almost touch your right leg.

4. Swing from your shoulders and arms, setting a slight angle with your wrists going back. Keep the swing neat and compact, encouraging a positive strike with little follow-through. The big mistake here is to make too long a swing. The more compact the swing the less likely it is that you will lose your balance and mishit the shot.

FAIRWAY BUNKERS

The choice of shot to recover from a fairway bunker depends on your ability, the game situation and your personal preference. Careful shot assessment is essential and will require you to consider the following:

THE LIE OF THE BALL This greatly influences your club choice and the distance you can achieve. A very poor lie will require a lofted club to return the ball sideways back to the fairway and a better lie.

THE LIP OF THE BUNKER FACE Assuming the lie is good, your club choice is further dictated by the elevation necessary for the ball to clear the lip.

THE CONTOURS OF THE BUNKER The base of the bunker might not be flat, adding to the difficulty in playing a long shot. Toughest of all is the downhill slope which requires the use of a very lofted club. However, any moderate or severe sloping lie will need careful consideration and probably a sensible recovery rather than a bold shot at the flag.

THE DESIGN OF THE GOLF HOLE A solid contact with a club which clears the lip of the bunker safely is not the best shot in every circumstance. Consider the percentage shot which finds the widest part of the fairway, or leaves a full shot to the green which might be easier to control.

CONSIDERATION FOR A LESS THAN PERFECT RESULT You might not achieve a perfectly clean contact and solid shot. Evaluate whether you should aim to play the ideal shot to clear 150 yards of heavy rough before the fairway is reached, or cover the possibility of the ball flying only half this by aiming towards a wider part?

The approach to fairway bunker shots is not dissimilar to a shot played from grass. The ball is struck before the sole of the club contacts the powdery sand to preserve clubhead speed. Hold the grip lower down to

1. A medium iron being used correctly in a fairway bunker. Position the ball back in the stance, move your feet into the sand and hold the club a touch lower to compensate.

compensate for the amount the feet will dig into the surface to secure a footing. Position the ball further back in the stance than normal, opposite the middle of, or towards, the right foot, so encouraging your wrists to lead the clubhead into impact which will steepen its approach, ensuring a solid contact with the ball. This will tend to de-loft the club too, so allow for this in your club selection. The rules don't permit you to ground the clubhead at the address position. Feel the weight slightly favouring your left side.

The swing should be limited to three-quarter length, resisting the tendency to shift the upper body behind the ball and fully transfer weight. Not only should the weight start on your left side, it should remain there throughout to steepen the approach of the clubhead into impact. Use technique, not force, to play the shot, relying principally on a solid contact from the centre of the clubface.

There is one advanced technique which will help in gaining some extra distance from fairway sand. If you open the clubface of a longer iron you will get good elevation to clear the bunker lip and get some extra distance from the longer shafted club. The ball flight will be a left-to-right fade, so allow for this by aiming left. Anticipate a high shot because opening the clubface progressively increases the effective loft.

2. Use enough loft to ensure that the ball clears the face of the bunker. Every bunker shot is different, so make sure that you assess your options carefully before playing the ball.

3. In this case the shallow face to the bunker and the clean lie permits the use of a fairway wood.

2

3

CHECKPOINTS

● If in doubt, select a lofted club and play back to the fairway.

● Use a club with sufficient loft to clear the face.

● Position the ball centrally or behind the centre to ensure a clean contact.

● Limit your swing to three-quarter length for control.

LOWER AND HIGHER TRAJECTORY SHOTS

There are many occasions when a shot purposely hit lower is more preferable to a shot played at a standard trajectory; such as to gain distance when hitting into the wind, or when playing from beneath trees to avoid overhanging branches.

A medium or long iron should pose little trouble. The ball position must move to the right of centre, which in turn reduces the loft if the wrists stay in the same position as normal, the shaft now being angled forwards at the grip end. If the shot is to stay low, the wrists must arrive at impact considerably ahead of the clubface. Moving the ball back in

1. 'Punching' the ball out from underneath the overhanging branches of a tree using a medium iron.

the stance should be compensated for by turning your left hand to your right on the handle; if you fail to do this, the clubface will be open at impact. Place more weight on your left side at the address position and hold the weight there throughout the swing. This will force an early setting of the wrists going back, and a rather steep approach into impact for the clubhead, driving the ball low and forwards, the clubhead really thumping into the turf.

There are fewer situations that demand a purposely hit, higher shot. The most obvious situation is when a tree is between yourself and the green. Instead of selecting a more lofted club, it might be advantageous to stay with the lower number and adjust your swing to produce a faster rising shot.

Driving downwind is another occasion when a higher shot is more suitable, making full use of the conditions to maximize distance. Tee the ball up a touch higher than normal. Position the ball opposite your left heel and move up to 75% of your weight distribution to the right side. Your right shoulder will feel lower and your left noticeably higher. The resulting swing will ascend though the hitting area, really driving the back of the ball both forwards and slightly upwards, the loft of the driver doing the rest. However, remember that this shot requires considerable ability to achieve a better result than if you were to stand and swing normally.

The higher trajectory shot from the fairway must be tackled another way. Because the ball is not teed up, an ascending clubhead at impact is of no use – it would contact the ground before the ball or thin the shot. The clubhead must still be descending at impact as normal in order to ensure the same ball/turf contact. A higher trajectory is achieved by opening the clubface at the address position and returning it this same way at impact. An open clubface increases the loft, thus dictating a higher flight. More height usually means less distance, so selecting one less lofted club would compensate. An open clubface will tend to hit a small slice or fade, so aim left to compensate. Whilst a lofted iron will move only slightly left to right, if at all, longer shafted clubs will cause the ball to drift much more.

2. Position the ball back in the stance and limit the backswing length.

3. A more lofted club has been selected to play over this tree which is blocking the path to the flag.

4. To add height to the shot, open the clubface a little, positioning the ball opposite your left heel.

CHECKPOINTS

● To produce a lower trajectory, position the ball back in your stance, your hands staying ahead and your weight on the left side.

● Hinge your wrists early and lead into impact with your left hand, hitting sharply downwards.

● For higher tee shots tee the ball up higher, put more weight on your right side and hit the ball on the upswing.

● For higher fairway shots, open the clubface up, align yourself left to compensate and allow for a fade.

WINDY CONDITIONS

1. To lower the ball's trajectory, position the ball back in the stance.

CHECKPOINTS

● With crosswind shots, imagine a target to the left or right and play towards it.

● Skilled golfers shape the ball to nullify the effect of the wind.

● Into the wind, select a less lofted club and play the ball back in your stance.

● When putting in a strong wind, widen your stance and position the ball central to your feet.

When playing shots through crosswinds you can either allow the ball to move with the wind, or learn to shape the ball flight to nullify its effect. The latter requires a high degree of skill, so the majority of golfers are best advised simply to judge the wind conditions and allow for them in their choice of club and aim.

In a left-to-right crosswind, visualize a target to the left, aim your clubface there and align your body so that it is parallel to this target line. Should the ball be unaffected by the crosswind, the next stroke is playable to the green, and should the ball be caught by an extra gust, it will still find the right of the fairway, or at worst the light rough. Remember that all allowances for crosswinds should be made entirely at the address position.

2. Widen your stance when putting in windy conditions to assist stability over the ball.

3

3. Punch the ball forwards on a lower flight by keeping your weight left and using an arms and shoulders action.

4

4. Hit the ball from right to left to lower the flight, keeping the ball beneath the full force of the wind.

A golf swing is a dynamic action that demands good balance at all times. That's a tall order with the wind buffeting your back or hitting you from the side. To counteract the problem, select a less lofted club, widen your stance a little to gain stability and use a three-quarter length backswing. With a swing like this there's less likelihood that you will lose balance, and the lower trajectory flight is affected less by the wind.

Hitting into the wind the main problem is distance loss. A slice or hook will be exaggerated, so if you are generally inaccurate you must be aware of this. You will require two or three more clubs than normal and a change at your address position. Position the ball further back in your stance and compensate by fractionally strengthening the left-hand grip. Your objectives are a lower trajectory, less backspin and, in dry conditions, to run the ball onto the putting surface.

Swing mostly from the arms and shoulders, limiting the use of the hands and wrists, which will scoop the shot upwards. Use of the lower

body is also restricted, principally because the weight will not have fully shifted to the right side in a shortened backswing.

Skilled players may choose to hook gently or draw the shot by aiming down the right side of the fairway and encouraging an early rotation of the right hand over the left before impact. This can be recognized by the clubface partly facing the ground halfway into the forward swing. The ball will curve from right to left in flight. The closed clubface at impact reduces loft and results in a penetrating shot.

Playing downwind, the conditions are more favourable but, while those drives could travel far, approach shots may run through the green. You will need to consider the best route to a flat landing area well before the green so that you can run the ball onto the putting surface. Select a more lofted club and swing normally thereafter. If you tend to be inaccurate off the tee, remember a tailwind usually reduces the effects of side spin on the ball, so here's your opportunity for a long drive.

The Short Game

THE SHORT GAME

There are four elements to golf's short game: putting, chipping, pitching and greenside bunker play. Each requires the correct application of the clubhead at slower clubhead speeds, the regulation of your backswing length and a slower tempo.

Very few golfers practise their short game enough, and devote most if not all time to the full swing. Whilst this may be more enjoyable, it can be fairly unproductive compared to short game practice. All short game shots require relatively little practice, once the fundamentals have been learned, as the swing is shorter and there are fewer movements to

2. Greenside bunker shots are simply an extension of the pitching stroke, although a cushion of sand should be removed at the base of the swing arc.

1. Develop your putting by experimentation.

control and co-ordinate. The shorter the shot, the more attention must be paid to detail.

The short game is progressive and each swing is an extended or shorter variation of another. Start with putting. This is a miniature version of your full swing, not a completely separate game. You need to stand closer and change your posture to aid control. The swing is mechanically simple, arms and shoulders moving back and through together. A minute amount of wrist action keeps the change of direction fluid as the forward swing begins. As you move to chipping, the same stroke is required. Adapt for a lofted club, weight on your left side, to nip the ground away immediately after the ball. The swing is an extension of your putting stroke, with slightly more right wrist hinge. The backswing length regulates the distance the ball travels, with a gentle acceleration in your forward stroke to stabilize the impact and provide consistency.

As you move to pitching, use an address position similar to chipping, weight not so much to the left side, but introducing more wrist action going back, your right hand folding back on itself to encourage your left hand to lead into impact. Again, regulate the distance by the backswing length.

Finally, to greenside bunker shots. The key to successful bunker play is to learn how to pitch successfully from grass first. Make a three-quarter length swing at a fairly slow tempo, nipping out a small divot past impact. Adjust the strike in bunkers to remove a couple of handfuls of sand, some prior to impact to cushion the strike. If you approach your short game this way, you will see that one good stroke lends itself to the next. Indeed, errors are often not isolated to one shot but exist in all short game departments.

Look not to the differences between the shots, but more to their similarities. There is a gradual setting of the wrists as the backswing length progresses. The only time wrist action needs to be eliminated is with short putts. Always make a backswing short enough to encourage a positive forward swing, not a deceleration of clubhead speed which is certain to be destructive to the strike.

Above all else, practise your shorter shots. They require familiarity with swing technique, but a little experimentation with the fundamentals can develop your short game. Once a swing is learned and grooved, you will always require some practice to maintain 'feel' and touch, but a tidy short game is the easiest route to lower scores.

3. Shots played from near the green require thought and imagination to picture the best shot for the situation. Remember that a lower, running shot is preferable to lofting the ball into the air. It is less susceptible to a poor first bounce and requires a smaller swing.

CHECKPOINTS

- All short game shots require the backswing length to be regulated to match the distance of shot.
- Your right hand folds back on itself when putting, and gradually more as the swing length progresses.
- Stand closer to the ball for shots requiring finesse.
- Encourage gentle acceleration through impact.

SETTING UP TO PUTT

A successful putting stroke must control direction and distance. Most of the necessary directional control is established at the address position by the use of a good aim and a square body alignment.

The putter face must be square to the target line. However, from above the ball this can appear distorted, so have your putter face aim confirmed by someone standing behind the target line, looking over the ball and towards the hole. From the front view, looking into a mirror, your putter shaft must be vertical or just fractionally angled forwards, hands leading.

A grip which limits any hinging of the wrists, especially the left wrist prior to impact, is preferable. The left hand should ideally be turned to the left of its normal position until the thumb locates fully on the flat fronted section of the club's handle. As the wrists are arched up for putting, the club will be stabilized by the left wrist and lower arm, which will assist putter face control in the stroke. The palm of your right hand should fully face the target, whilst the thumb will locate beneath the left and again fully on the flat section of the club's handle.

The most frequently used grip is the reverse overlap. The left forefinger locates outside the four fingers of the right, further assisting to firm up the left wrist and prevent this breaking down just prior to impact. All four fingers of the right hand are against the handle, with no additional overlap or interlock. This putting grip is most easily

1. Keep your eyes over the ball when putting – drop another ball to confirm your position.

- ● Establish a square putter face first, checked by a friend to confirm.
....
- ● Try a reverse overlap grip to firm up your left wrist.
....
- ● Stand closer to the ball, your upper body more over the ball.
....
- ● Find your most comfortable width of stance, wider being more stable than narrow.
....
- ● Align your body parallel to the target line.

2. Position yourself with the ball close to your feet and slightly to the left of centre.

3. Arch your left wrist upwards.

adapted from the baseball grip by repositioning the left index finger and turning the left hand to its better position left of neutral at the same time. An overall light grip pressure enables you to sense the precise movements involved.

Stand closer to the ball than for a normal stroke, whilst bending both elbows towards your body and out slightly until they very lightly brush your sides. Create the space to move the putter back and through by raising your wrists upwards. Your upper body will need to lean more over the ball, until the back

of your neck faces skywards. Maintain some flexibility in your knees to restore the balance between toes and heels, preventing your weight shifting onto the toes due to the angled upper body position.

From the front view, the ball should be located forward of centre in the stance to encourage a sweeping action of the putter head. The sole of the putter should be moving parallel to ground level or slightly ascending at the point of impact.

Position your eyes directly over the target line when putting. Comfort should dictate the width of your stance but roughly shoulders' width apart is ideal, your weight evenly distributed both between toes and heels and left and right sides. Turn your toes fractionally out – perhaps as much as 10 degrees – to assist balance.

The best chance you have to return the putter squarely at impact, as it coincides with the target line, is to adopt a square stance.

THE PUTTING STROKE

The putting stroke originates from the arms as they pivot around the swing centre located at the base of your neck, central to your shoulders. Throughout the swing, the angles formed at the address position must be maintained. Neither arm should be allowed to straighten even slightly. Keep your head still throughout the putting stroke, as head movement is the most common cause of poor contact and direction. You almost have to listen for the ball to drop into the hole, resisting any temptation to see the result.

Work at rocking your shoulders up and down in response to the arm movement caused by taking the putter back and through. Try to hold your legs absolutely still throughout, pivoting from the centre point of your shoulders. Introduce a slight hinging of your right wrist going back; this maintains the stroke's fluency and prevents a stop and change of direction at the backswing's completion. The putter should sweep back low to the ground and remain close past impact.

CHECKPOINTS

● Don't push the sole of the putter into the green. Instead, let it move slightly up and down, lifting just prior to swinging back.

● Tap your putter head very gently up and down at the set-up, to prevent tension creeping in.

● Try to keep your lower body and head absolutely still to promote the most effective stroke.

● Keep your putter moving low both back and through to roll the ball forwards to the hole.

1. Take the club back in one motion, arms and shoulders moving together with just the slightest hinging at the right wrist to aid fluidity in the stroke.

2. The forward stroke should be longer than the backswing. Your left wrist must be in control and your lower body should remain still.

The putting stroke is a small version of a full swing with a lofted club. It follows a path which travels slightly around the body in the backswing, along the ball-to-target line at impact, and slightly around again in the follow-through. Simple enough in theory, but with very short putts you may feel as though the stroke is straight back and through.

You must not force the putter back straight when it should naturally move inside the line, nor must you attempt to hold the clubface square to the target throughout. Just allow the putter head to follow its most natural track.

Your putting stroke must have the correct pace to it. The backswing should be slightly shorter than the forward stroke, and the putter must gently accelerate through the ball. It will feel as though it is 'one-third back, two-thirds through' as you keep the backswing smooth and easy, but the forward stroke positive. Don't allow your putter head to decelerate through impact.

Your left wrist must remain firm throughout impact and beyond. If this breaks down prior to the strike, the putter face will turn left. The left hand leads the putter, but your right hand principally controls the 'feel' to the stroke. Work at pushing the putter forwards with the palm of your right hand, holding each forward stroke to ensure that the left wrist has remained constant.

Your putting stroke is individual, and ultimately you have to find a formula that works for you. Experiment with a longer, slower stroke, which is particularly useful on middle to longer distance putts. Try a shorter, tapping action, usually better for short putts.

DRILL Try using a ball marker, located underneath your ball to focus your eyes on a fixed point. The ball marker should encourage your head to remain absolutely still throughout the stroke. It is important to avoid any tendency to lift up or move towards the target as this would disrupt the putter face control. Use 3 golf balls on the practice green, positioning each ball over a marker pushed fully into the ground, to cause no disruption to the roll. Strike the putt and keep looking at the marker, listening for the ball to find the bottom of the hole.

3. Allow the putter to move on a gentle arc both back and through.

4. Position your ball over a marker to keep your body still.

PUTTING –
DIRECTION AND DISTANCE

Direction control when putting is based primarily on putter face control. The putter face dictates 90% of the direction, assuming a flat putting surface and a square aim at the set-up. The path of the putter through impact – its swinging direction – has a 10% influence.

Focus on your putter head. As your backswing starts, the face will turn just slightly away from the target, return squarely for impact and continue to turn to the left of target. Remember the ball and putter head are

in front of you and your putting stroke moves around your spine, as in every other swing. As your shoulders have to rock and turn as part of the overall mechanics, so the putter face must respond. However, it is incorrect to manipulate the putter face throughout, keeping it square to the target line. Permit the putter face to open and close – but it will square up for impact. The question is, how much should it deviate from the target line? Adopt your set-up, no club, elbows brushing

your sides and palms facing each other. Keeping your knees stationary, rock and turn your shoulders from side to side, roughly mimicking your putting stroke. The hands follow your shoulders and should turn away from the target if you hold your elbows in. Now try working your right elbow away from your side in the backswing, directing your palm more at the target. This works your arms independently from your upper body, leading to all manner of inconsistencies at impact.

1. Try using another ball as a backstop to encourage gentle acceleration through the shot.

Every golfer has more difficulty with distance than direction. Most three-putted greens are caused by the first putt finishing short or rushing past the hole. Never lose sight of the fact that you have an allowance of two putts per green. Your first putt should roll the ball close, leaving you with a simple tap-in, and distance is most often the key to this. Long putts holed are a bonus!

There are two aspects here. Firstly, you have to read the green, looking at the slopes around the putting surface, trying to judge the predominant contours. You should also try to assess the texture of the grass and the speed of the greens.

Secondly, your putting stroke must be capable of adjustment to vary the distance. This is not purely 'feel', but instead requires a variation in mechanics. The easiest way is to combine a variation in your swing length with the pace of the stroke. For a short putt, limit your backswing length to permit a gentle acceleration through impact, whilst working

at a slower tempo. For longer putts, extend your swing, adding a faster pace to the stroke.

With practice, you should be able to match your backswing length to the distance

you want the ball to roll, thus having additional control when trying to assess the variations in swing length needed for uphill and downhill, fast greens and slow.

2. The putter head should follow a gentle arc on all putts, though this will be less apparent on shorter putts.

3. Don't try to work the putter straight back, as this encourages the arms to work away from the body and reduces your control over the shot.

CHECKPOINTS

● Check your putter face aim and alignment.

● Move your putter on a very gentle arc around your body both back and through.

● Let your putter face move away from facing the target going back – it will return squarely for impact.

● Match your backswing length and overall tempo to the distance.

THE 3-METRE 'FEEDBACK' PUTT

1

1. 10 feet (3 m) is the ideal distance to practise your putting; it enables you to easily monitor your results and correct the basics.

Putting is best developed with three golf balls placed some 10 feet (3 m) from the hole, on a level or very slightly uphill section of the practice green. Most of your putting practice should initially be from this distance until the basics are grooved into place. Position a ball marker or coin to ensure you start from the same place each time. Place the golf balls alongside one another and move across to each one in turn. As you putt, a pattern is certain to emerge. You might be holing out fairly consistently with those that miss, passing just alongside the edge and finishing just one foot (30 cm) past. This represents an ideal speed to maximize your chances of holing out, slow enough to permit a ball touching the edge to fall in rather than lip out of the hole, yet fast enough to ride over any minor imperfections in the putting surface, especially those adjacent to the hole.

This 'feedback' putt allows you to analyse and adjust accordingly. Once a pattern has emerged, identify key points to work on to solve the problem, as follows.

FREQUENTLY SHORT Backswing too short. Check your backswing is long enough to permit a gentle acceleration through impact, without having to apply a conscious hit. Try a slightly longer backswing.

No acceleration. The putter head must accelerate through impact to maintain control and produce consistent speed. Ensure your putter head passes through impact and travels further, going through to promote acceleration.

Unsolid contact. The ball will only roll its full distance if it is struck from the 'sweet spot' on the putter face – this is usually represented by a centre line. Your putter might be too light; experiment with other models and weights.

BALL FREQUENTLY MISSES LEFT Clubface aiming error. Check that you are square to begin; in particular you should check the position of the putter face and your shoulder line.

Left wrist firmness. Your left wrist must remain constant through impact in order to control the putter face. However, if the wrist hinges prior to impact, the face of the club will close.

Backswing putter face control. The face should normally turn slightly away from the target in the backswing as the inside path dictates. If you attempt to hold the putter face square to the target line throughout the backswing, it will turn to the left for impact.

BALL FREQUENTLY MISSES RIGHT Aim and alignment. The most common error is to align your toes to the hole; this dictates that the putter face is aimed to the right. In the correct position your toes should be parallel to the target line.

Poor putter face control. The putter face should turn away from facing the target going back, but anything more than a very slight wrist action will roll the putter face open. Keep the putter face looking at the ball longer.

Left wrist control. If your left wrist leads too much through impact, the putter face will be forced open. Use your right hand to 'feel' the directional control.

BALL FREQUENTLY ROLLS TOO FAR PAST OR SPINS OUT Backswing too long. Shorten it by practising using a backstop, such as another ball, to encourage a more compact stroke.

Acceleration too aggressive. Apply a gentle acceleration, with a smooth change of direction as the forward stroke commences.

Putter too heavy. Try other models with lighter head weights.

Tempo. Slow the whole stroke down and try to keep it smooth.

2. This backswing is too wristy – arms and shoulders should move more.

3. A common putting error – the left wrist has collapsed prior to impact.

PUTTING DRILLS

Putting drills are used to make you more aware of the 'feel' of a particular movement or strike of the ball, so improving your overall ability on the greens. Putting is principally about control and 'feel', the mechanics of the stroke being of less importance once the basics of aim, grip, body alignment and the basic stroke have been mastered. Use your practice time effectively, making use of a variety of drills. Try out these putting drills and measure their relative value by sticking with each for at least 10 minutes. If you feel you have enhanced your control over the putting stroke following a particular drill, build this into your regular practice sessions in the future.

DISTANCE Middle to long-distance putts require more attention to be paid to distance than to the line. Try looking at the hole whilst taking several practice putting strokes, sensing how the stroke will 'feel' without actually looking at the putter or the ball. This should help to develop your 'feel' for the putt ahead by moving your conscious thoughts away from the length of the backswing or the pace of the putting stroke.

LISTENING FOR THE DROP Many golfers lift up too early, not just looking up but raising their upper body fractionally even before the ball is struck. Use three golf balls, putting the first to the hole having looked at the line and distance. Putt the next two without looking up, so that you can recognize the stroke required without necessarily seeing the result each time. Learn to listen for the ball to drop into the hole. Use golf balls numbered differently and putted in sequence to assist your analysis of the results.

1. Practise putting to three distances on the flat area of a green, marking each distance with the shaft of an iron club. Try to stop the ball immediately in front of the shaft you are aiming for. Vary the distances you putt to, so that you can improve your control over shots on the green.

2. Line up a number of balls on sideslopes. Start with the nearest and work back to develop the feeling for how the ball will 'break' or curve depending on the pace you put on the shot.

NINE-BALL DRILL Space nine balls in groups of threes at equal distances to each hole on the practice green. Alternatively, lay iron shafts down at three distances on the green. Select three distances that are roughly 15, 30 and 45 feet (5, 10 and 15 m) away and putt at random to each. Monitor your progress by trying to make every putt finish level with the intended hole. If you have shafts laid down on the green, try to stop the ball immediately in front of each shaft. Since this is a distance-only drill, rather than a directional drill, use a flat area of the green initially.

UPHILL AND DOWNHILL Try a drill that enhances 'feel' on a sloping section of the practice green. Putt three golf balls uphill and then reverse the direction. Try to find a section of the green where there is little or no sideslope, and ideally where you can practise putts of 20 feet (6 m) or more. Comparing the extremes of additional pace for the uphill putt and added touch going downhill is a valuable way to promote better control.

SPOKE DRILL The most awkward distance is 3–6 feet (1–2 m), short enough to expect to hole out, long enough to require a sound stroke and absolute control. Arrange a number of balls around a hole on the green, initially on a level section. Move around the circle of balls and count the number holed in a row. Progress to a gently sloping section to add further interest, giving a variety of uphill, downhill and sideslope putts.

CHECKPOINTS

● Try looking at the distance while making practice strokes to 'feel' the backswing length required.

● Listen for the ball to drop, holding your body position until well after impact.

● Putt to different distances on the practice green, either by selecting different holes or laying shafts down.

● Use the 'spoke drill' to develop your short putting skills, counting the putts holed successively.

3. The 'spoke drill', shown here, is most effective when practising shorter putts.

4. Try putting with only your right hand on the club; this will develop your 'feel' for putter face control.

CHIPPING

Low, running shots can be valuable around the green. The basic chip shot, using a 7-iron on a level surface with normal conditions, will have roughly 30% 'air distance' and 70% 'ground distance'. Adopt your normal grip, but turn your left hand a touch right, introducing another half or full knuckle when viewed from the front. This left-hand adjustment will compensate for the change in the position of the wrists, as they are pushed forwards at the set-up. Your right hand must fully face the target. The shot requires touch and control, so adopt a grip with a light-to-medium pressure which encourages the correct freedom for the swing action.

Hold lower than normal on the club, so that your right index finger almost touches the shaft of the club itself. This assists with control over the clubface and enables you to stand closer to the ball at the address position.

Position the golf ball opposite the centre of a fairly narrow stance, or even slightly to the right of this. Try keeping your heels about 8 inches (20 cm) apart. Your right foot is best kept at 90 degrees to the ball-to-target line, but angle the left toe out some 20 degrees.

Push your wrists forward until the butt end of the club coincides with your left thigh. At the same time, position two-thirds of your weight over your left leg and slightly kick in your right knee. This lower body position and weight distribution must feel reasonably

1. The basic chipping stroke comes, principally, from the arms and shoulders.

2. Gently accelerate in the forward stroke.

3. Practise with another club to encourage your left wrist to lead into impact and beyond.

4. Hold your swing position after every shot to make sure that your weight has remained on your left side.

CHECKPOINTS

- Use a 7-iron, which will fly the ball about one-third of the distance. The remainder is along the ground.

- Hold lower down on the club for control, pre-set the weight to the left side and use a pendulum-type swing with the arms.

- Try to keep the body quite still throughout the stroke to preserve the quality of the ball contact.

- The correct chipping stroke will gently accelerate the clubhead through the hitting area. Keep your backswing quite short and work at a positive strike.

comfortable as each remains constant while the swing motion takes place.

By standing closer to the ball than for a full swing and by holding lower down on the club, your right elbow should lightly brush your stomach or side. Your left arm will be a touch more extended as it forms more of a straight line with the club's shaft.

The chipping stroke should involve as few moving parts as possible, ideally limiting any action from the lower body and instead using the shoulders and arms together. Excessive use of the wrists or hands will disrupt the clubface control and lead to inconsistencies in the strike and direction.

Develop the correct pace for the stroke through practice swings. Remember it as 'one-third pace going back; two-thirds pace

through impact.' Rhythm is important. The swing motion must be smooth, not robotic. Your wrists will most naturally hinge at the completion of your backswing and remain so for impact and beyond.

Try to brush the ground lightly at impact or fractionally beyond, certainly cutting some blades of grass or removing a very shallow and small divot on longer chip shots. Take plenty of practice swings and try to grow accustomed to this impact.

Hold your through swing position after every shot and check that you have maintained your spine angle throughout, only rotating your head to see the result. Check that your body weight has remained on your left side, even pulling your right heel off the ground on longer chip shots.

ADVANCED CHIPPING

The average golfer should limit the choice of clubs for chipping to a 6-or 7-iron, as they produce predictable loft and roll. However, the more skilled player should experiment with other clubs. Club choice is principally governed by the optimum point of the first bounce – far enough onto the putting surface to avoid the ball tangling with the fairway grass or semi-rough, short enough to turn a lofted shot into a running ball. Remember, it's easier to control a running ball.

Use the chart to picture various shots around the green, applying the optimum air distance and percentage of distance on the green:

4-iron	10% air distance	90% ground distance
5-iron	15% air distance	85% ground distance
6-iron	20% air distance	80% ground distance
7-iron	25% air distance	75% ground distance
8-iron	30% air distance	70% ground distance
9-iron	35% air distance	65% ground distance
Pitching wedge	40% air distance	60% ground distance

Large, undulating greens require a wider range of chipped shots. A 4-or 5-iron giving little flight and plenty of run is particularly useful when there is a two-tier green and the ball must run up to the higher tier. A downhill chip shot requiring the most delicate of strokes is best played with a wedge or 9-iron, adding a touch more loft and spin to prevent the ball racing by the flag.

With the 8-and 9-iron and wedge, position the ball a touch further back in your stance, opposite the right heel, and ensure the back of your left hand leads throughout. If it does not, the right hand will flip the ball into the air, resembling a pitch shot.

The shaft lengths of the 4-and 5-iron make them awkward to control, and require your hands to move to the lowest section on the grip. If you keep your hands leading throughout, the protruding grip will not catch against you. Play these shots centrally to the feet, weight just favouring the left side, and sweep the ball off the turf with a putting-type action, limiting the wrist hinge to a minimum in the backswing – for shorter distances, use no wrist hinge whatsoever.

The ideal club choice to maximize control for shorter distances is a 6-or 7-iron. Stand much closer to the ball and grip at the lowest section of the handle. Arch your wrists upwards, which in turn should push your elbows in until they lightly brush your sides. Your upper body posture should be lower, ideally bringing the eyes into a position directly above the ball. The reverse overlap grip, as recommended for putting, is ideal for this type of shot.

The sole of the clubhead will not fully ground, its heel clearly raised due to the ball being much closer to your feet. Position the ball opposite the toe end of the clubhead as the intention is to strike it from this spot. The result is a deadened impact and the ball taking off less fiercely. Try a narrow stance but angle the left toe out around 30 degrees whilst drawing it back from square. Keep your left wrist just ahead of the clubface at the address position.

The stroke originates from the shoulders and arms. There is a small hinge of the wrists as the backswing nears completion, further encouraging the left wrist to lead the clubface into impact. The success of this shot relies on the left wrist position being retained during impact and beyond. There should be enough freedom to hinge going back and maintain fluidity in the stroke, but no opportunity to release this for impact. In this way, your swing can be bolder and is less likely to fail you in pressure situations.

1

2

CHECKPOINTS

● During club selection, consider the distance each club will move the ball through the air and along on the ground.

● Move the shorter irons back in your stance to encourage a slightly steeper swing.

● Hold less lofted irons lower on the grip, keeping your hands forward to prevent the grip catching against you.

● For shorter shots, try adapting your chipping to mimic your putting stroke, and use a reverse overlap grip.

● Employ an arms and shoulders action, hinging a little from the wrists as the backswing progresses.

1. For shorter pitching use a reverse overlap grip – left forefinger outside the right hand, wrists arched up and the arms closer to you.

2. Employ a putting type action when chipping. The swing should be mainly from your shoulders and arms, with little use of the wrists.

3. Take a fairly short backswing, with the clubface close to the ground. . .

4. . . . followed by a slightly shorter forward stroke with a gentle, but positive, acceleration.

3

4

PITCHING

The general rule of thumb is to run the ball to the hole when the situation permits, but greenside bunkers, grassed banks and contoured greens will often dictate a higher, soft-landing shot. For this type of shot, club choice is limited to either the pitching wedge or sand iron (if it has a small flange).

Aim your clubface squarely to the ball-to-target line. Adopt your normal grip, keeping your grip pressure light. You may wish to hold slightly lower down on the handle to help maintain control. The golf ball is played central to your feet, the stance being quite narrow. Balance the weight evenly between the feet, and evenly between toes and heels too

for maximum stability. Tilt your shaft more towards the target in order to encourage your left wrist to lead into impact. Start with your shoulders aligned in a position parallel to the ball-to-target to ensure a good swing direction.

The pitch is simply an extension of the chipping stroke, the only real difference being at the address position. The backswing starts with the right shoulder turning away whilst the arms swing back. The path of this swing is slightly around the body – rather than straight back from the ball. Your wrists should begin to hinge straight away going back, the right folding back on itself to point the toe end of the club vertically at

1. The ball is positioned centrally within a fairly narrow stance, the weight is evenly spread and the player's hands are placed fractionally ahead of the ball.

2. The wrist angle must be set early on in the swing, with the right wrist folding back on itself as the shoulders turn away towards the right side.

halfway back, your right elbow folding close to your side. Your shoulders will have turned about 40 degrees at this position.

Now reverse the backswing to return to the ball for impact, with the key movements being the co-ordinated arm swing and body turn. Continue past the contact point into a forward swing which is a right arm extension, your left elbow working gradually behind you in the forward swing. This has the effect of maintaining clubface control through impact, resisting any chance for the right hand to close the clubface. The shoulders turn around 70 degrees to the target side at the completion of the follow-through. Again, there must be weight transference, this time onto your left side, half raising the right heel and pulling your knee across. Good weight shift moves the lowest point in the swing just beyond the ball to ensure a solid contact before the ground is brushed.

This swing will feel like an underarm throw, the principal idea being to keep the palm of the right hand facing the target longer.

Although roughly equal in length, the backswing must be relatively slow and smooth, the downswing positive, almost brisk. There is little chance of success with a long laborious swing, so keep it compact, keep it simple and accelerate that clubhead.

---

3. A typical pitching situation, with a bunker between the player and the green. The clubhead must move around the body, whilst the toe end of the club is directed skywards with the right elbow folding away.

CHECKPOINTS

● Use a pitching wedge, or better still, a sand iron with a narrow bounce sole with little flange.

....

● Play the ball centrally to a narrow stance, your weight just favouring the left side.

....

● Align your shoulders squarely and angle your lower body towards the target up to 20 degrees.

....

● Your right wrist must fold back on itself early into the backswing.

....

● Keep the clubhead accelerating through impact, transferring the weight over to the left side.

ADVANCED PITCHING

Certain situations around the green demand creative shotmaking skills. Once you can pitch successfully with a square clubface, you should adapt your swing to vary both the height and resulting backspin on the ball. Select a wedge or sand iron; the latter should have a narrow sole and shallow flange.

Take a situation with the hole cut close to the edge of the green, a bunker intervening. The ball must have enough height to land softly and run little. Try opening the clubface, turning it more to the right. This increases the loft angle. To compensate for this, align your body to the left, particularly your shoulders, as they do most to dictate the shape of the swing to follow. Rotate your hands to the left on the club to prevent the clubface from returning square at impact.

The swing will follow the line of the body, back outside the normal path and returning the same way. It will move left of target through impact, your body being encouraged

1. The player hinges his wrists early while going back, in order to encourage the left wrist to lead throughout the downswing.

2. Accelerate the clubhead through impact, arms and body moving together, weight transferring to the target side to ensure a solid, clean contact.

to turn and your weight to shift positively to your target side. Hinge your right wrist back early in your backswing and lead with your left wrist throughout your downswing and beyond. Your left elbow must fold behind you, not to the ground, if you are to hold the clubface open. Make a longer swing to compensate for the higher flight and slow the whole swing whilst still providing some acceleration through the ball.

Anticipate the ball bouncing just a touch to the right on landing because of the sidespin created by the open clubface. Practise this shot from a variety of distances. It is an asset to your short game, especially when playing to small, heavily bunkered and harder greens.

A steep upslope requires careful shot assessment. Don't automatically reach for your pitching wedge or sand iron. The upslope will increase the loft of the club, sending the ball steeply into the air. The

3. This practice drill helps promote vital clubhead control. Use your right hand to 'feel' how the palm must work under the club to hold the clubface skywards.

CHECKPOINTS

- When opening the clubface, align your body, particularly your shoulders, to the left to compensate.

....

- Your swing must follow the line of your body, the club-face being open to this for impact.

....

- Steep upslopes may require a less lofted club.

....

- Lean into the slope and fold your arms past impact to keep the club moving through.

better club choice may be a 9-or 8-iron. Also consider the position of the flag and how much green you have to work with.

A steep upslope around a green leaves no option but to 'punch' the swing into the slope, cutting the follow-through short. However, you must still accelerate the clubhead through impact and not quit on the shot.

The address position is formed with the weight set more to the left side, leaning into the slope in order to gain stability and balance. The hands should be pre-set slightly forward to encourage a descending strike. The swing is mostly from the arms, with your body kept steady to maintain balance. After impact, the club will hit the grassy upslope, and your arms will 'give' to allow the club to follow the slope.

This is a shot worth practising because it takes confidence to know you can hit it quite hard and the ball still might not pass the flag. The effect of the slope on the loft of the ball will take a while to grow accustomed to. The sin is to leave this shot well short of the hole.

APPROACHING THE GREEN

1. From 70 yards (64 m), use a three-quarter length backswing.

2. From 40 yards (36.5 m), limit your follow-through, but still shift your weight.

Your full swing with a sand iron will hit the ball up to 90 yards (82 m), giving a very high trajectory and plenty of backspin. If the flag is closer, you must adapt your swing technique to limit the clubhead speed, so controlling the distance. Use your pitching wedge or sand iron, the latter ideally having limited flange and a narrow sole.

70 YARDS (64 METRES) This distance requires a three-quarter length swing. Hold the club as normal, clubface square to the target, shoulders parallel and with a narrow stance. Keep your hands ahead of the clubface with your weight favouring the left side and your left toe angled out a touch to assist stability. Encourage an early hinging of your wrists, your right hand folding back on itself quite early with the feeling of a narrow, steeper swing. Your right elbow should remain close to your body with your left arm comfortably extended but not straight or rigid. Limit your backswing length and shoulder turn, then gently accelerate down and through the ball, nipping out a small divot just beyond. Follow through enough to mirror your backswing length. Resist your right hand crossing over through impact and instead encourage your left elbow to fold behind you slightly, though not downwards as in a full swing. This keeps the clubface directed at the target longer. You should feel as though you are sitting down at, and after, impact, your knees remaining flexed even at the completion of the swing. The ball-turf

sequence at impact relies on a good weight transference. Keep your right knee flexed going back and let it pull through towards the target in response to your hips turning left as you swing through.

40 YARDS (36.5 METRES) From 40 yards (36.5 metres), your swing should be based on feel, rather than swing mechanics. Touch and feel shots are reliant on your right hand control, your left wrist remaining firm through impact, but your right sensing the distance. Hold slightly lower down on the grip, coming closer to the ball and adopting a narrow stance. Position the ball opposite your right instep, hands ahead, and keep your weight pre-set on your left side throughout. Lower your wrists towards your left thigh and

CHECKPOINTS

● From 70 yards (64 m), restrict your backswing but still accelerate throughout your downswing. Keep your hands slightly ahead, hinging your wrists early in your backswing.

● From 40 yards (36.5 m), shorten your backswing to encourage acceleration as the swing reverses. Position the ball back in your stance and feel that the stroke is controlled by the right hand.

3

4

open your stance a touch to create space for your arms and club to swing freely through impact. Keep both your clubface and shoulder line square and swing positively up and down. Hinge your wrists early going back as your right elbow works close to your side. Turn your shoulders to encourage an inside path to the swing, limiting the backswing length. From here you must accelerate, your arms and right knee working towards the target as your upper body remains still. Resist your right hand and lower arm crossing over and instead work your left elbow behind you as it folds. This directs the clubface skywards and keeps your right hand in control, feeling the distance. Develop the feeling of a good pitching action – set the right wrist angle early into the backswing, then preserve this in your downswing. You will have to shift your weight to the target side, your right knee moving across to create sufficient room for your arms to swing through.

3. From 40 yards (36.5 m), limit your backswing length, as this encourages positive acceleration throughout the downswing.

4. From 70 yards (64 m), continue until the club is over your left shoulder, ensuring your weight has fully transferred to the target side.

GREENSIDE BUNKER SHOTS

The best way to visualize a greenside bunker shot is to think of the ball being 'splashed' out along with a couple of handfuls of sand. The club will not necessarily contact the ball, but the cushion of sand will 'float' the ball out and onto the green. It should not be a steep chopping action, or an 'explosion' shot.

Use a suitable sand iron, one designed to 'bounce' through the sand, preserving clubhead speed. Look for a clubhead shape that has a rounded leading edge, 58 degrees of loft and a broad sole. The sole should have a slightly pronounced flange which will raise the leading edge off the ground. This club will cut through the sand without the need for excessive force – a sharper edge would just dig downwards.

Don't let the sole of the club touch the sand at your address position or as the club swings back, as this would 'test the surface of a hazard' and would incur a two-stroke penalty in stroke play.

Position the ball opposite your left heel; your weight should be evenly distributed, with a stance wide enough to keep you in balance throughout. Shuffle your feet slightly into the sand in order to secure a footing. Hold slightly lower down on the grip to compensate for this. Your swing action must be principally arms and shoulders, your right wrist folding back on itself early into the backswing to create a steeper backswing.

By opening the clubface at address, perhaps 15–20 degrees, the effective loft of the clubface is increased, leading to a higher shot that lands more softly. The ball will also fly to the right of the hole, so the entire body must be aligned to the left to compensate. The resultant swing shape will now move across the ball-to-target line on an outside-to-inside path. However, it is not necessary to contrive this swing shape as your shoulder line dictates it.

1. Use a long enough backswing…

2. …to remove a couple of handfuls of sand.

The sand removed prior to impact will create resistance, slowing the clubhead speed. You must allow for this by making a slightly longer, more positive swing, brisker in pace than from grass and with the intention of mirroring your backswing length. A bunker shot to a hole 20 yards away will require a swing length equal to a 40-yard pitch shot played from grass. Practise this from grass first, then take the swing into the bunker and remove the sand before the ball.

TIP In the practice bunker, use a circle or ellipse drawn around the ball to develop the ideal strike. The sand within the shape will be roughly two handfuls. Focus on the back edge and hit out the sand within this shape. This may take considerable practice, but it provides you with an good 'picture' of how the club must work under the ball through impact.

4. The key to good bunker play is to remove a decent amount of sand.

3. Let the club continue on its course well beyond impact.

CHECKPOINTS

● Splash the ball out, removing a couple of handfuls of sand.

● Don't ground the club at the address position, as this would infringe the rules.

● Use a swing length twice that for the same shot played from grass.

● Make a brisk swing and ensure the follow-through is as long as your backswing.

CONTROLLING DISTANCE FROM SAND

There are several ways that you can successfully influence the distance of shots from greenside bunkers. These techniques provide the necessary range of shots for all situations. Work towards finding a combination of techniques that can be easily applied out on the course. Keep things simple, as it is important to be able to picture the type of swing necessary for each shot.

CLUBFACE The more you open the clubface prior to the swing, the higher the ball flight, the greater the rate of backspin, the more the ball will tend to kick to the right on landing and the shorter its distance. As you square the clubface or turn it fractionally closed, the flight will be lower, the ball will bounce straighter and go further, assuming the swing is identical and the amount of sand removed equal.

SWING LENGTH If you shorten your swing length the clubhead speed generated for impact will be reduced, and the ball flight will reflect this. By making a fuller swing, clubhead speed is considerably increased and the ball travels further. This assumes, of course, that you keep the clubface position constant and splash out the same amount of sand with each shot you play.

1. Opening up the clubface increases the loft, giving the shot more loft and less distance.

2. Longer bunker shots require just a small amount of sand to be removed prior to impact.

3

3. The ball is tight to the lip of the bunker, and there is only a short distance to go to the hole, so a short backswing is needed.

4

4. A good shot. Plenty of sand has been taken, cushioning the impact and popping the ball into the air and on the green.

5

5. From this position, tight to the lip of the bunker, there is little room for the forward swing.

SAND REMOVAL Consider three identical swings, each with the clubface some 20 degrees open, each with the ball positioned left of centre in the stance. Now put an imaginary circle – 9 inches (23 cm) in diameter – around each ball. The clubhead is to enter the sand at the same point each time, represented by the back of this circle. If the ball were located in the centre of the circle of sand, the ball would fly 20 yards (18 m). If it was located further forwards in the circle, the ball would fly a shorter distance as there would be more clubhead resistance prior to impact and more of a sand cushion for the ball flying a shorter distance. If the ball were back in the imaginary circle, little sand would be removed prior to impact and the ball would fly further due to the reduced resistance.

ANGLE OF APPROACH The regular greenside bunker shot is played with the ball positioned just forward of centre in the stance. This is the base point in the swing, where the swing arc is at its lowest. If you move the ball further back in the stance, centrally or just right of centre, the clubhead will still be descending as it makes contact with the sand. The wrists will lead into impact, de-lofting the clubface and lowering the trajectory of the ball flight.

If you wanted a shorter, softer landing shot you would move the ball position closer to the left foot. The same swing will be more shallow, contacting plenty of sand prior to the ball and encouraging more height. The latter is reserved for skilled golfers as it is hard to judge the swing length compensations

necessary. However, it is a suitable shot from a clean lie on a gentle upslope or flat area.

CHECKPOINTS

● Open the clubface to increase the loft and reduce distance. Close it for the opposite effect.

● Vary the amount of sand taken according to the amount of clubhead resistance required.

● Move the ball forwards in your stance to add height for shorter shots.

BUNKER UPSLOPES AND DOWNSLOPES

1. Stand as perpendicular to the slope as is possible without losing balance, widening your right foot to help gain a decent stance in the loose sand. Swing back wide and from the arms and shoulders.

Some bunker shots will require you to adapt your normal stance and stroke to ensure you finish close to the hole.

UPSLOPES For the gentle upslope your body angle should be as perpendicular to the slope as possible, your shaft should be inclined back a touch and the ball located slightly more forward than normal. This increases the loft, so don't open the clubface much unless quick height is required. Too open a clubface will pop the ball up without enough forward flight toward the hole. Adopt a wider stance to assist your stability, and feel more weight on your right side, your left shoulder noticeably higher. Swing normally from here, adding a little to the length of your swing to compensate for the increased loft. Still remove sand before the ball, working the loft of the clubface under the ball to give it the necessary height. Stay behind the shot, your head remaining in position until beyond the moment of impact. Don't lean into the shot by moving your head towards the target – the swing will steepen and the clubhead will dig in too deeply.

The steeper upslope bunker shot is less controllable, with its severity dictating that you have to lean into the slope, upper body angled fractionally to your right side. Find the most comfortable position, with your right leg slightly bent and your left foot angled out and up the slope. Your swing cannot match the slope so the clubhead will have to cut into

2. The correct position, with the ball opposite the right foot, from which to play this difficult shot.

3. Pick the club up very early going back, in order to steepen the angle of the downswing.

the sand just behind the ball, taking very little sand before impact and preserving clubhead speed.

DOWNSLOPES One of the hardest shots in golf, the downhill bunker shot requires a few vital stance and swing adjustments. Move the ball back a touch in your stance, open the clubface quite wide – around 30 degrees – and stand as perpendicularly as you can to the slope. Your left shoulder should be lower than normal, weight on your left side and your toe angled out to give stability. Hinge your wrists quite early and try to remove a shallow cut of sand – similar to that taken from a level stance. Try to keep the clubhead following the downslope contour, resisting any tendency to lift up prior to the strike, which would top the ball or give a thin contact. Limit your backswing length and gently accelerate through impact, focusing your eyes on the point in the sand where the clubhead must first strike.

The steeper downslope is thankfully a rarer shot. Your first objective is to extract the ball from the hazard in just one stroke, without compounding the problem by skimming the ball over the green into worse the other side. Careful shot assessment is vital. Open the sand iron face wide, position the ball opposite your right foot and angle the

shaft forwards, hands well ahead to dictate both a steep backswing and approach to the ball. An early wrist hinge is essential to further steepen the backswing; then feel your left hand pull the club down and through, making as low a forward swing as possible whilst maintaining your balance. Angling your left foot out at around 45 degrees and widening your stance will assist your stability.

CHECKPOINTS

- On gentle upslopes, angle your body perpendicular to the slope and swing normally, extending your normal swing slightly.
....
- Stay behind the shot, following through up the slope.
....
- Lean into more severe upslopes to retain balance. Swing steeply and hit into the sand just before the ball.
....
- Move the ball back in your stance and stand perpendicular to the slope.

SIDESLOPES IN BUNKERS

BALL BELOW FEET The ball below the level of your feet is particularly difficult, as judging the right amount of sand to take is hard. The only consolation is that the swing is generally shorter, so you can achieve greater control. You are forced to hold at the very end of the club, standing closer to the ball and ideally open with your lower body to encourage a steeper swing action. Leave enough room to swing past your right knee, testing with a couple of trial backswings. Widen your stance and sit a touch more at your knees, lowering yourself so that you can reach the back of the ball with ease. Your upper body must be inclined forwards more, bringing your head into a position almost over the ball. From here, you have to maintain this upper body posture as this is the key to hitting just the right amount of sand. Stay down as you swing, concentrating on keeping your head at the same level throughout, resisting the tendency to lift up mid-swing.

The ball is likely to fly a touch to the right because the shaft is tilted more upright at the address position, so angling the clubface that way. Combine this with a slightly open clubface for the shot, established at the address position, and you will have to aim to the left in order to compensate. The steeper swing action will require a longer backswing as well as positive acceleration throughout your downswing.

A shot that demands improvisation is when the ball lies in a greenside bunker well beneath the level of the fairway but with no

room for you to stand. Each situation must be evaluated individually, but most involve finding a footing which is fair according to the rules – you must not build a stance – and finding some way of positioning your feet to retain balance at least until impact.

BALL ABOVE FEET This is the easier of the sideslope greenside bunker shots. Hold the club lower down – on the very base of the grip just above the shaft itself. You will be forced to stand further away to accommodate the wider swing that results from the shaft

1. The ball below the feet – the harder of the two sideslopes. Try to stay down throughout the backswing, keeping your head at the same level and tilting the left shoulder towards the ball.

angle flattening at your address position. Your posture should be more upright than normal, though it is important to maintain the bend at the knees. The ball will take off to the left because the clubface loft is inclined that way when the lie angle is flattened. Aim to the right – roughly 20 degrees – to compensate, though this will vary depending upon the severity of the sloping lie. Use either a square or slightly open clubface.

Your swing must still remove a shallow cut of sand which cushions the ball at impact and controls its distance. This swing will be mostly arms and shoulders, with no opportunity to pivot fully, no apparent weight transference and very little use of the wrists in the backswing. Your upper body angle must remain constantly upright as you move your arms back and through, removing the normal amount of sand. Anticipate a lower ball flight

because the clubface is closed, thus reducing the loft angle. Allow for more bounce and run on the ball, making this shot tough when the flag is close to the edge of the bunker.

CHECKPOINTS

● Ball above: hold the grip lower down.

● Ball above: aim to the right to compensate for the loft angle directing the ball to the left.

● Ball below: bend over more from your hips at set-up and aim to the left of your target.

● Swing from your arms and shoulders, maintaining a constant spine angle.

● Take a shallow cut of sand to cushion the strike.

● Maintain your upper body posture throughout and stay down until the ball is struck.

2. With the ball above the feet, stand further away from the ball and grip the club lower down.

3. Swing slowly, from the arms and shoulders and remove a shallow cut of sand.

HALF-BURIED IN SAND

If the bunkers at your course have soft sand, you've probably experienced your fair share of half-buried lies. The number one objective is to extract the ball from the hazard in just one stroke. Number two is to control the flight and roll of the ball and finish up near the flag. There are usually two options when playing from a half-buried lie. Deciding which to take depends upon distance from the flag and the amount of green available.

OPTION 1 Most bunker shots from a half-buried lie are relatively short in distance and most greenside bunkers are in depressions where the shot must have enough elevation to clear the lip. Select your sand iron and lay the clubface wide open – as much as 30 degrees. Position the ball more towards your right foot, thereby setting your wrists forwards. Align your body some 20 degrees left of target to allow for the ball coming out in the direction of the clubface. Angle your left toe out more

1. The ball must be positioned towards the right heel. The hands should remain well ahead of the ball, with the weight to the player's left side.

2. Take the club back steeply, cocking the wrists early on. Clubhead speed is generated mainly from your arms as you hit down, with the left hand leading through the shot.

than normal and sit just slightly through that knee with the weight most positively on the left side.

Use a steep swing, descending into the sand 2–3 inches (5–7 cm) behind the ball. The idea is to turn the sole of the club at the heel into the leading edge. This narrowed section leads as the clubhead enters the sand, reducing resistance and retaining sufficient clubhead speed to

3. Use the sole of the clubhead, at the point at which it meets the rounded socket, to nose underneath the ball. The swing must be very steep and powerful to allow for the resistance of the sand at impact. You must also be precise enough to strike the sand well before the ball, allowing the clubhead to dig the ball out from the sand. Any follow-through will be limited as the clubhead buries itself into the sand.

clear the hazard. The swing is easy enough if you have set-up correctly. The backswing will be a steep, picking-up action, mostly from your arms, wrists cocking upwards very early. Make a full backswing and then hit firmly down with the feeling that the left hand is leading all the way. Most of the time the clubhead buries itself in the sand, but you must try to pull it through to a short follow-through. Accelerate the clubhead all the way, your concentration and focus solely on the point behind the ball where the club enters the sand.

OPTION 2 If the distance to the flag is more than 20 yards (18 m) and the lip on the bunker is small, this second option might prove successful. This shot will fly very low and run a considerable distance. Turn your sand iron or wedge about 15 degrees closed at the set-up. Align your shoulders some 10 degrees to the right of target, your hips and feet parallel to the target line. Keep your hands forwards and the weight mostly on your left side. The wrists will return ahead of the clubhead, combining with the weight distribution to deliver a steep, almost chopping action as the clubhead approaches the sand in the downswing. Resistance is minimized because the sharper, leading edge of the club is turned so that it enters the sand first, clearing a path for the wider part of the blade to follow.

You will require a fairly complete backswing to generate sufficient clubhead speed for impact, but limit the shoulder turn, thus encouraging the club to swing straight back. There's no chance of any follow-through with this shot and the clubhead will stop in the sand beyond where the ball was positioned.

CHECKPOINTS

● Open the clubface wide and move the ball back in your stance.

....

● Move your weight left and swing steeply up and down, hitting the sand hard just before the ball.

....

● If you have green to work with, close the clubface and chop steeply down into the sand behind the ball.

Trouble-Shooting

VIDEO CAMERA USE FOR GOLF

Many people own or have access to a video camera, making it possible to view their golf swing, and even to slow it down or freeze a frame to check and analyse the position. Many instructors have invested in video equipment.

There is no doubt that a high-quality playback of a golf swing can be enormously beneficial to all players, but bear in mind that a video playback cannot replace an instructor explaining a particular point and positioning you correctly. The mental picture and physical sensation of the swing must come first.

If you are keen to use video to assist your improvement programme, there are key features to look out for in your equipment selection. First of all, a fast golf swing requires the option of a shutter speed of at least 1/4,000 of a second, and preferably up to 1/10,000. Secondly, the format of the camcorder should ideally be high grade, offering some 400 lines of resolution. More sophisticated camcorders feature still frames, but a 'clean still' is most beneficial, the picture being a clear stationary position. Ask your dealer to recommend a quality format.

Forward and reverse, preferably at a controllable speed, is best achieved by reviewing using a VCR with a jog shuttle. A hard copy print-out is available by linking the VCR to a video printer. These additions are hardly cost effective for one person to buy, so seek out a golf instructor who uses video and has invested in this equipment.

The camcorder requires plenty of quality light at high shutter speeds. Choose a sunny day. Use a tripod to keep the picture still. Camcorders which rest on the shoulder are easy to steady. Otherwise use a hand-held model with a 'picture steady' feature, which removes the rapid shaking so common with compact models.

Be consistent about the location of the camcorder. When shooting from behind, position it exactly between the toe line and an extension of the target line. From the front, make sure it is face on, and at the same

1. Place the camcorder on a tripod, making sure that it is always at the same height so that you can compare the results of your practice sessions.

2. Shooting your videos from face on enables you to check the position of the ball in the stance, the position of your hands at the set-up and the position of your head.

height and distance away each time. Try ten paces in each direction, at a height of one driver shaft length. The ball or feet should be at the very base of the picture. Have some practice swings first to ensure the whole swing fits, checking in the viewfinder. Try to use a contrasting background such as trees when shooting face on, to make the picture as clear as possible and give reference points. Shoot a few swings from each angle, talking into the microphone and describing the ball flight and quality of contact. Review the swings initially at normal speed. Since we are accustomed to seeing only good swings on TV, the initial impression might disappoint. It can, of course, work the other way too, giving you a confidence boost to see your orthodox swing. Use dry wipe markers on the screen to highlight key points.

ERADICATING THE SLICE

The slice is one of the most common and costly errors in golf. The less lofted clubs, the driver in particular, cause the greatest problem. The slice is caused by an open clubface at impact, which imparts sidespin on the ball causing it to curve away once the initial velocity has eased in mid-flight. With the driver, the reduced backspin cannot hide the slice, the ball curving away near the peak of its flight.

The key lies in the role of the lower arms and wrists as the club approaches impact – the right arm and wrist must rotate over the left, squaring the clubface for the all-important moment of impact.

You should check two important items when trying to eradicate the slice. Use a 6-or 7-iron initially, and ensure your clubface is square at the address position. Now check your grip. The correct position for the left hand is indicated by two and a half knuckles in view when you check in a mirror. The right hand should be positioned so that your right thumb conceals your left, with your palm facing the target. A slicer's grip will position one or both hands too far left, so that as the hands find their most natural or 'neutral' position for impact, the clubface opens, causing the slice.

Check the clubface position in your swing by moving it through three stages, initially stopping at each. At halfway back, with the club shaft parallel to the ground, the clubface should be at 11.30 on an imaginary clock face as you are viewing it. The toe end of the club should not be

1. A typical slicer's grip: both hands are turned too much towards the player's left. As the hands revert to their most natural position at impact, the clubface will open.

2. Adherence to the 'straight left arm' principle will force the clubhead to remain open through impact and beyond. At this point the toe end of the clubface should be facing straight up.

3

3. In the correct position the left wrist should form a flattish line with the left forearm. However, here it is concave, causing the clubface to open at the top of the backswing.

4

4. This practice drill will help to promote the arm rotation that squares the clubface up at impact. Draw your right foot back and feel your right hand turn over before impact.

vertical; rather the clubface looks out and a touch downwards. Should there be a grip error or an early rotation of the wrists, the clubface will now be looking more skywards. Continue to the top, and start down slowly until the club shaft returns to the same position, where the clubface must be reviewed just prior to the release action. Check for that same leading edge alignment at the 11.30 position on the clock face.

Now for the key movement: the right hand and lower right arm must begin to rotate over the left, taking with them the whole body turn. The body will follow the action of the arms, hands and club if the grip pressure and body tension are light. Maintain this lower arm and hand rotation until the club shaft has reached parallel to the ground in the forward swing, at which point check that your right arm is now the extended arm and your left elbow has begun to fold or is just about to. The toe end of the clubhead is directly upwards. Rehearse this sequence, with particular emphasis on the cross-over through impact.

The slicer locks wrists and lower arms through impact, leaving the clubface open. The resulting halfway through position directs the clubface skywards, often with the left arm rigid, instead of folding away to accommodate the continuation of the follow-through.

CHECKPOINTS

● Check your aim and grip first. One or both of your hands could be excessively to the left on the club.

....

● Don't lock your wrists and lower arms prior to impact – this will deliver an open clubface.

....

● Cross your right hand and lower arm over your left to square the clubface.

CORRECTING THE HOOK

The typical hooked shot not only curves to the left, but bounces and rolls in this direction, eventually finishing in trouble. The hook is not restricted to the longer clubs, as the sliced shot tends to be. You can hook as effectively with a lofted iron as with the driver.

To cure yourself of this problem, first check your clubface alignment, ensuring the leading edge is at 90 degrees to the ball-to-target line. Take great care with your grip, because many hookers of the ball need only alter their hands on the club to solve the problem. Check your hands in a mirror or lift the club up in front of you to look down on them. A grip associated with the hooked shot will be positioned too much to your right showing three, or more likely all four, knuckles of your left hand. The palm of your

right hand is probably underneath the shaft too much, instead of facing the target.

If your aim and grip are correct, swing to halfway back and check your clubface control, shaft parallel to the ground. The leading edge of the clubface should point to a position equivalent to 11.30 on a clock face. A closed clubface will be indicated by that edge pointing more to the 10 o'clock

position. Have you been trying to keep your clubface square to the target going back? It should, in fact, rotate gradually as your backswing progresses. Encourage your right elbow to fold away and feel your right hand fold back on itself quite early.

Now to the top of your backswing, where your left forearm and the back of your hand should form an almost straight line to

1. An example of a typical hooker's grip – both hands are to the player's right.

2. The anticipation of the hook often encourages the player to aim to the right of the target. Here the shaft, at the top, has been aligned too far to the right.

preserve clubface control. Swing back, stop and look until you are familiar with the feeling of this position. In comparison, a closed clubface looks mostly skywards, the back of your left wrist being convex, thumbs to the side of the shaft, not underneath.

The technically correct position at halfway down will return the clubface leading edge back to 11.30 on the clock face – check for this – and then continue past impact into the forward swing. At halfway through the toe end should be vertical, but if it has rolled closed, the face will be directed forward to the ground, indicating your right hand and lower arm are rolling over the left excessively. To correct this, try keeping the clubface looking at the target past impact, keeping your left arm extended longer.

To accelerate the learning process, hit shots with a 7-iron, holding the back of your left hand at the target much longer and resisting the right hand crossing over. It will take considerable practice to overcome the previous habit of the clubface returning closed, so be realistic and work at it in gradual stages until it becomes second nature.

3

CHECKPOINTS

● Check your grip first. Ensure your left hand shows no more than two and a half knuckles, and that your right palm faces the target.

● Rotate your wrists going back, to point the toe end of the club skyward.

● Restrict the crossing over of your wrists through the hitting area.

● Feel the back of your left hand pull towards the target to resist your right hand crossing over.

● Encourage a swing direction moving left of the target through impact from outside to inside.

3. To correct the hook, try practising swinging to the left leaving the clubface open. Remember that a hooked shot is caused by a closed clubface at impact whilst the swing direction generally moves to the right of the target, from outside-to-inside. Try using a control exercise to promote the feeling of doing the opposite, so correcting the error quickly and efficiently. The only problem may be an over-correction, though initially this should not be a problem. Use a medium iron, certainly not a long iron or a wood. Take several practice swings with the idea of both aligning your shoulders to the left of target at the address position and swinging along an outside-to-inside line. Resist any temptation for your right arm to turn over the left, and instead keep the back of your left hand working towards the target for as long as possible.

TOPPING AND THIN SHOTS

Dispense immediately with the idea that you 'must keep your head down' to correct topping. Your head, in itself, will not lift up too early because your brain is programmed to watch the ball. The golfing world is full of those who spend time on practice grounds trying to keep their head down, when the origin of the error lies elsewhere.

There are fundamentally just two ways to top the ball. Lifting your spine angle is the first of these. To combat this, establish your address position, positively angling your upper body forward whilst flexing slightly at your knees. Feel as though you are pushing your backside outwards and slightly concaving your lower back, keeping your head up and away from your chest.

You have now established the single most important angle for the swing: the spine angle. Set it at the address and maintain it throughout the swing. This spine angle forms the axis around which your upper body can pivot freely. Complete your backswing and feel as though your left shoulder is lower, but not so low that it is angled directly towards the ball as this would be tilting. The shoulders must turn at 90 degrees to your spine, your upper body angle remaining unchanged.

Starting down, use your arms and lower body, again maintaining a constant upper body angle. At three-quarters through, your right shoulder will be lower having worked its

1. Buckling the arms inwards shortens the swing radius causing you to top the ball.

2. Poor posture. The upper body has lifted – a very common error.

way underneath and around your chin. You must feel as though you have really stayed down on the shot until the ball is well on its way. From here on, your right shoulder will gradually lift as your right arm extends fully, swinging up to the completion of the follow-through. The golfer who habitually tops shots, thinking his head is lifting, is most likely raising his entire upper body. This naturally causes the head to lift, but the lifting of the head is a symptom and not a cause of the problem. The spine angle lift is the error.

The second principal way of topping shots, assuming the spine angle is constant until well beyond impact, lies in your swing radius. This is the extension of your left arm and club shaft, originally set at your address position. In your backswing, your left arm should be comfortably extended, permitting your wrists to hinge. This extension is maintained until past impact, after which your right arm becomes the extended arm as the left gradually folds away. In this respect, the golf swing can be understood as a two-sided action. Shorten this radius by bending your left arm going back or pulling both arms inwards nearing impact, and you will surely top or thin the shot.

You have to learn to swing the golf club positively downwards during the downswing, as part of a free-swinging action. Take practice swings with a medium iron, trying to remove a shallow divot at the base of the swing arc. Since centrifugal force is trying to pull the clubhead into the correct arc or orbit as you provide the swing motion, the sole of the club should brush the grass away.

---

3. If the wrist leads into impact, the shot will be topped as the swing radius is shortened.

CHECKPOINTS

● Work at setting a good spine angle at your address, and maintain it during your swing.

....

● Feel your left shoulder is low going back, your right lower going through to stay in the same posture.

....

● Swing your arms downwards freely to let the sole of the club remove a shallow divot.

....

● Try to extend your left arm going back, your right arm past impact.

CORRECTING PUSHED AND PULLED SHOTS

The pushed shot flies straight, but to the right of the target. To produce a pushed shot the swing direction at impact must be from inside-to-outside and the clubface must additionally be open to the ball-to-target line, roughly at 90 degrees to the swing direction.

The pushed shot is most often the result of a faulty backswing. If your shoulders over-rotate, particularly early in your backswing, the shaft will align to the right of target at the top, crossing over. To correct this, check your shaft is parallel to the target line at halfway back and then really swing the arms upwards, limiting your shoulder rotation. The shaft will feel 'laid off' at the top, aligned to the left of target.

Assuming the club is positioned correctly going back, you have to look at your movements as you reverse the swing. Stop your club at hip height in the downswing and look at the position of the shaft. It should be parallel to the ball-to-target line or, as you will view it, coinciding with your toe line. From here onwards it will approach the ball on an elliptical path from around the body and travel along the ball-to-target line for a short distance at impact before continuing on an arc around the body in the forward swing. This is the ideal swing direction which is associated with straight shots. By contrast, the swing which will push the ball to the right of target will drop the shaft excessively 'inside' the ideal shape, first seen halfway into the downswing. From this position it moves

1. Incorrect. Right shoulder is too dominant.

2. Correct. The arms swing the club down.

CHECKPOINTS

● Check your shaft alignment at the top. Prevent it crossing over from parallel to the target line.

● Don't force the club back too straight from the ball.

● Turn your shoulders more going back and hit from the inside path.

on an inside-to-outside path and continues to the right of target.

A shot is 'pulled' when it flies straight, but to the left of the target. At impact the swing direction is moving across the intended ball-to-target line from outside-to-inside. In addition, the clubface must be angled to the left, or closed, but is roughly square to the swing path. A pull will fly lower than a straight shot because the outside-to-inside swing direction tends to steepen the clubhead's approach into impact, effectively de-lofting it slightly. With tee shots, this may well cause the occasional skied shot too.

Check your address position first, paying attention to your shoulder alignment, which should be square but may be open, so forcing both your backswing and downswing to move across the intended line, pulling the ball left. Assuming your set-up is correct, you may be forcing the clubhead rather straight back from the ball instead of letting your right shoulder turn dictate more of a rounded shape. Too straight a backswing forces the shaft to misalign at the top, pointing considerably left of target.

The most common error leading to a pulled shot is to unwind your upper body – most notably your right shoulder – prematurely, casting your arms away from your side and failing to drop your left arm downwards. With the shoulders now out of position, your arms have no choice but to swing from outside-to-inside. You can check this by stopping at halfway down. The shaft should be parallel to the target line, but with a pulled shot the shaft will be outside the line, moving across the line through impact and continuing excessively left of target. Correct this by re-routing your downswing, dropping your arms more to the inside path and feeling the shaft follow through to the right of target.

3. An outside-to-inside swing direction moves the shaft left of the target.

4. Correct the fault in pic 3 by swinging more towards the target.

SHANKING AND TOE END CONTACTS

A shank occurs when the ball is partially or wholly struck from the neck of the club. With an iron, the ball will fly severely to the right, and far enough to end up in plenty of trouble. The equivalent shot with a wooden club will fly very low and left.

1. If the arms swing downwards in the plane, the clubhead will move through impact on a consistently good path. The strike will be solid and the ball will gain good distance.

Most golfers who shank also tend to slice, fade or pull shots. Shanking and slicing are both caused by the clubface being returned to the ball wide open. There are primarily two causes of this error, the first being an over-rotation of the hands early in the backswing, fanning the clubface open. Secondly, your wrists could lock up prior to impact, leaving the clubface wide open, usually accompanied by your right side dominating, unwinding too early in response and causing the clubhead to return further away from where it started back.

The other type of shank is more directly related to your swing plane than the clubface. Hitting a golf ball forwards involves moving the club both around yourself and up and down, the combination of which is called swing plane. Keep the club moving in a constant plane throughout your swing and you will hit the ball solidly from the centre of the clubface. If you change your downswing plane so that the clubhead returns further away than at the address position, you will shank the ball. The most frequently seen error causing this is at the very

CHECKPOINTS

- Check that you are standing at the correct distance from the ball. Using a medium iron there should be roughly 8 inches (20 cm) between your left hand and thigh.

- Maximize your stability by distributing your weight evenly between toes and heels.

- Do not over-rotate your hands early in the backswing.

- Prevent your right shoulder moving round early in the downswing.

- Shanking a pitch shot usually occurs when you set-up open and roll the clubface early in the backswing.

start of this downswing, the right shoulder initiating the movement, forcing the club on a downswing path that is wider and more shallow than in the backswing. The body weight is thrown onto the toes at impact, and the ball is shanked. Once again you notice the connection between slicing, pulling and shanking. The typical first movement in the downswing of the golfer who slices or pulls is this right shoulder moving out too early to compensate for the error. Ultimately, this produces an outside-to-inside swing direction.

No error is as infuriating as the shanked pitch shot with some 40 or 50 yards, or metres, to the flagstick. The error occurs due to the downswing plane being flatter than the backswing plane, the clubhead returning further away from you than where it started at the set-up.

One way this develops is by standing open with the shoulders at the address position, but rolling the wrists early in the backswing. This not only flattens the plane, it sets the wrists in a position from which they are likely to stay locked through impact, leaving the clubface open too. To correct this, square the shoulders up at the address position and work at preventing the right shoulder from moving around early in the downswing. Promote the downward swinging of the arms and feel as though you will be striking the ball from the toe end of the clubface.

2

3

2. The shanked pitch results from the right shoulder being thrown around too early into the swing. Try to swing through and check that it has held back, as shown.

3. This practice drill is intended to prevent shanking by promoting the arms, rather than the right shoulder, as the club starts down. Address the far ball, but re-route the downswing to the nearer ball.

INDEX